SpringerBriefs in Psychology

SpringerBriefs in Behavioral Criminology

Series Editor

Vincent B. Van Hasselt, Fort Lauderdale, FL, USA

Behavioral Criminology is a multidisciplinary approach that draws on behavioral research for the application of behavioral theories and methods to assessment, prevention, and intervention efforts directed toward violent crime and criminal behavior. Disciplines relevant to this field are criminology; criminal justice (law enforcement and corrections); forensic, correctional, and clinical psychology and psychiatry: neuropsychology, neurobiology, conflict and dispute resolution; sociology, and epidemiology. Areas of study and application include, but are not limited to: specific crimes and perpetrators (e.g., homicide and sex crimes, crimes against children, child exploitation, domestic, school, and workplace violence), topics of current national and international interest and concern (e.g., terrorism and counter terrorism, cyber crime), and strategies geared toward evaluation, identification, and interdiction with regard to criminal acts (e.g., hostage negotiation, criminal investigative analysis, threat and risk assessment). The aim of the proposed Briefs is to provide practitioners and researchers with information, data, and current best practices on important and timely topics in Behavioral Criminology. Each Brief will include a review of relevant research in the area, original data, implications of findings, case illustrations (where relevant), and recommendations for directions that future efforts might take.

More information about this series at http://www.springer.com/series/10850

Roxanne Heffernan • Tony Ward

Dynamic Risk Factors for Sexual Offending: Causal Considerations

Springer

Roxanne Heffernan
School of Psychology
Victoria University of Wellington
Wellington, New Zealand

Tony Ward
School of Psychology
Victoria University of Wellington
Wellington, New Zealand

ISSN 2192-8363 ISSN 2192-8371 (electronic)
SpringerBriefs in Psychology
ISSN 2194-1866 ISSN 2194-1874 (electronic)
SpringerBriefs in Behavioral Criminology
ISBN 978-3-030-58274-6 ISBN 978-3-030-58275-3 (eBook)
https://doi.org/10.1007/978-3-030-58275-3

This Springer imprint is published by the registered company Springer Nature Switzerland AG
The registered company address is: Gewerbestrasse 11, 6330 Cham, Switzerland

Preface

Dynamic risk factors (DRF) are the children of risk prediction. They were identified to help practitioners assess the risk of recidivism and then became treatment targets for interventions aiming to reduce this risk (Andrews & Bonta, 2010). The *predictive* nature of their legacy lies in their ability to provide reliable information about the likelihood of future reoffending. In this respect, DRF are useful complements to static risk factors such as age, gender, and history of offending and add incremental validity to recidivism prediction (Hanson & Harris, 2000). Their *treatment* utility resides in the fact that practitioners increasingly rely on the identification of DRF to direct correctional assessment and interventions. In their book, *The Psychology of Criminal Conduct*, Andrews and Bonta (2010) use the term *criminogenic needs* to refer to those DRF that "when changed, are associated with changes in the probability of recidivism" (p. 49). In other words, they are viewed as potential causal factors that if effectively targeted by cognitive-behavioral techniques will reduce reoffending rates. In a similar vein, Mann, Hanson, and Thornton (2010) identify a number of DRF, which they believe to be prima facie causes of sexual offending and validated predictors of recidivism. They refer to these factors as *psychologically meaningful risk factors* and propose that: "the causal factors for sexual recidivism will ultimately be drawn from variables similar to those included in our list. We believe that it is these variables that should be emphasized in treatment" (Mann et al., 2010, p. 210). These include DRF such as deviant sexual interests, offence-supportive attitudes, lack of emotionally intimate relationships with adults, emotional congruence with children, lifestyle impulsivity, poor cognitive problem-solving, and general self-regulation problems (Mann et al., 2010).

Thus, in the correctional psychological literature, DRF have a dual status. They are viewed as: (1) useful predictors of reoffending and measures of risk status and (2) potential causes of reoffending, capable of serving an explanatory (i.e., causal) role as well as a predictive one. It is a simple and powerful conceptualization that has streamlined forensic and correctional research, program development, and the delivery of treatment. Despite its conceptual elegance, we believe that the dual conceptualization of DRF is fundamentally flawed and at best they can only function as *markers* of causality rather than being causes themselves (Ward, 2016; Ward &

Beech, 2015; Ward & Fortune, 2016a). If this assertion is true, then two questions arise: What role, if any, should they play in the development of explanations of crime (and reoffending)? And how can they assist practitioners in treatment?

In this book, we address these two questions. First, we argue that the focus of explanatory theories in the forensic and correctional fields should be on causal mechanisms. Second, we propose that DRF should not be regarded as causes of crime because they cannot be coherently conceptualized as causal mechanisms and are best viewed as composite or summary constructs referring to processes, states, and entities. Third, the question of how best to move from risk factor to causal status is examined and a number of methodological guidelines are suggested. Fourth, a conceptual framework for identifying the causal elements in crime-related problems is introduced and its application to DRF is outlined. Finally, we discuss how best to utilize DRF in assessment contexts and intervention programs. Our conclusions are that DRF are valuable predictors of recidivism and that they *can* serve an important methodological function in identifying the causes of crime and reoffending. They are boundary riders that inform researchers and clinicians about the existence of problems; they do not specify what these problems are or how they cause crime.

Contents

About the Authors

Roxanne Heffernan, PhD, MSc, is an Adjunct Teaching Fellow at Victoria University of Wellington, New Zealand and works in the field of correctional rehabilitation. Dr Heffernan completed her PhD in 2020; this research focused on developing explanations of offending based on human agency and applying these to correctional practice. She has published a number of academic papers on dynamic risk and protective factors and their relationship with human agency and crime.

Tony Ward, PhD, MA (Hons), DipClinPsyc, is a Professor of Clinical Psychology at Victoria University of Wellington, New Zealand. Dr. Ward has previously taught clinical and forensic psychology at Canterbury, Melbourne, and Deakin universities. He has over 440 academic publications and his research interests are offender desistance and rehabilitation, forensic and correctional ethics, and theoretical issues in psychopathology. His books include *Rehabilitation: Beyond the Risk Paradigm*, coauthored with Shadd Maruna (Routledge, 2007), *Desistance from Sex Offending: Alternatives to Throwing Away the Keys*, coauthored with Richard Laws (Guilford, 2011), and *Evolutionary Criminology*, coauthored with Russell Durrant (Academic Press, 2015). Dr. Ward is the developer of the Good Lives Model for the rehabilitation of offenders.

Chapter 1
Current Conceptualizations of Dynamic Risk Factors

Abstract Dynamic risk factors (DRF) are arguably the most important construct in forensic and correctional psychology. They are the basis of risk prediction and management, and the foundation of intervention programs aiming to reduce crime. In this chapter we outline a number of influential contemporary views of DRF. First, we define DRF and discuss the various types of crime-related factors. Next, we discuss their origins and conceptualization within the Psychology of Criminal Conduct (PCC), followed by a description of their dual roles in practice. Then we outline their place within explanations of offending, focusing mainly on theories of sexual offending. We conclude this chapter by highlighting the importance of developing explanations of offending which rely upon causal mechanisms. This chapter is intended to emphasize the reliance on these foundational constructs in correctional practice aimed at reducing crime and the research which informs these crucial tasks. This highlights the critical nature of questions about what exactly DRF are, how they relate to behavior, and how we should use them within treatment and risk management.

Keywords Dynamic risk factors · Risk prediction · Theories of offending

DRF can be defined as changeable aspects of persons and their environments which are statistically associated with higher rates of recidivism in offending populations, they predict rates of reoffending (Bonta & Andrews, 2017). They can be contrasted with static risk factors which also predict recidivism but are not able to be changed via intervention (e.g., age, sex, criminal history). DRF can be divided into those factors which are stable (i.e., change relatively slowly) and those which are considered acute (i.e., can change rapidly) (Hanson & Harris, 2000). The distinction between stable and acute factors is useful in guiding the day to day management of enduring vulnerabilities and responding to imminent risk (i.e., increases in risky

R. Heffernan, T. Ward, *Dynamic Risk Factors for Sexual Offending: Causal Considerations*, SpringerBriefs in Psychology,
https://doi.org/10.1007/978-3-030-58275-3_1

states or contexts). Theoretically, stable and acute DRF have been described as offence related vulnerability versus its manifestation in certain contexts (Beech & Ward, 2004). This view of DRF is known as a 'propensities model'; proposing that crime related traits (i.e., stable dynamic factors) may or may not lead to offending in various contexts (Mann, Hanson, & Thornton, 2010). For example, while an individual may have a propensity to use substances or violence to deal with their emotions (traits/propensities), risk is heightened when they experience intense emotions and/or are intoxicated (states) and in the presence of a potential victim. For this reason, stable DRF are most often the targets of intervention, they are thought to be enduring but changeable *and* causally linked with offending. Thus, in addition to being used to predict likelihood of reoffending, DRF are used as the targets of treatment programs aiming to reduce recidivism, they occupy *dual roles* in practice (Ward & Fortune, 2016). These roles are highlighted in structured risk assessment tools' evolution over the past four decades (see below), from initially containing primarily static risk factors, to incorporating dynamic variables which can estimate risk but also provide guidance for intervention. The use of DRF to classify individuals by risk level, allocate to treatment programs, formulate cases, and explain behavior is now standard practice (Heffernan & Ward, 2017).

1.1 Origins of DRF

Meta-analyses during the 1980s and 1990s identified a robust set of risk factors for crime (Andrews & Bonta, 2010; Bonta & Andrews, 2017). According to Andrews and Bonta (2010), these factors are crime correlates and predictors (i.e., statistically associated with reoffending), including dynamic predictors; a subset of these are conceptualised as potential causes of crime. Proposed causal dynamic predictors are called *criminogenic needs* (Andrews & Bonta, 2010), to reflect their relationship with behavior and their role in treatment. In *The Psychology of Criminal Conduct* (PCC), Andrews and Bonta (2010) state that criminogenic needs are DRF which "when changed, are associated with changes in the probability of recidivism" (p. 49). Andrews and Bonta (2010) identified a set of eight 'central' risk factors (seven are dynamic/criminogenic needs) which have the greatest empirical support in predicting reoffending: a history of criminal behavior (a static factor), antisocial attitudes, antisocial associates, antisocial personality pattern, marital and family factors, employment and school, leisure activities, and substance abuse. Andrews and Bonta (2010) recognize that these factors may be described in various ways by different researchers, for example, weak self-control, problems with self-regulation, or psychopathic traits.

Contained within the PCC is the widely used Risk-Need-Responsivity (RNR) model, which is built upon the predictive utility and presumed causal nature of DRF. The RNR is comprised of three main principles (and a number of less central ones); the risk, need, and responsivity principles (Bonta & Andrews, 2017). The *risk principle* states that risk can be predicted and that it ought to determine treatment intensity, higher risk cases should receive more intensive treatment, and lower risk cases little to no intervention. It is recommended that in order to increase predictive validity, both static and dynamic factors are assessed (Olver & Wong, 2019). The *need principle* states that treatment should target a range of criminogenic needs such as those listed above, relative to non-criminogenic needs (i.e., those which are not predictive of recidivism, e.g., mental health, self-esteem). The *responsivity principle* states that interventions should be responsive to the evidence concerning what works to reduce recidivism (largely cognitive-behavioral therapies) and the individual needs of the participants (e.g., literacy, mental health, cognitive capacity, motivation). The dual roles of DRF are reflected in these principles, they are both predictors of risk used to determine intervention dosage *and* criminogenic needs to target. There are additional principles within the broader RNR model, these will not be discussed here as they are less reliant upon DRF.

1.2 Prediction

As stated above, the primary role of DRF is to predict the probability of reoffending, both to manage risk and to determine the allocation of management and treatment resources (i.e., the risk principle). When DRF are present, rates of reoffending tend to be higher; they work as statistical predictors. The development of risk assessment tools is typically described as four generations evolving over the past few decades in response to the needs of the field (Andrews & Bonta, 2010; Bonta & Andrews, 2017). The first generation of risk assessment involved unstructured professional judgment, however, these predictions had poor accuracy and overall were no better than chance (Hanson & Morton-Bourgon, 2009; Hart, 2009). The second generation was the rise of 'actuarial' or numerical mechanical risk assessment, involving the aggregation of mainly static risk factors to estimate the likelihood of recidivism. Actuarial assessment was (and continues to be) more accurate in predicting recidivism. However, second generation risk measures are poor guides for intervention and fail to detect treatment changes and inform the ongoing management of risk, as they typically do not include DRF (Andrews & Bonta, 2010; Beech & Craig, 2012). The third generation of risk measures largely overcame the limitations of the previous generation by including the assessment of DRF within actuarial tools, thereby adding incremental validity to static risk assessment (Olver & Wong, 2019). The fourth generation extended the purpose of risk assessment from merely predicting risk to informing decisions relating to case management, for example the level of service/case management inventory (LS/CMI; Andrews, Bonta, & Wormith, 2010). The items in these risk assessment measures tend to correspond to the central eight (Andrews & Bonta, 2010; Bonta & Andrews, 2017). It has been suggested that a potential fifth generation may use more complex analyses and utilize machine learning to predict risk in the moment (Lovins, Latessa, May, & Lux, 2018).

Occurring alongside the emergence of actuarial assessment was the development of "structured professional judgment" (SPJ; Hart & Logan, 2011). As the name suggests, SPJ involves more judgment on the part of the practitioner in determining the presence and severity of DRF (Hanson & Harris, 2000; Hart & Logan, 2011), and in this sense it is less objective than actuarial approaches. It is a narrative approach, involving a comprehensive interview focusing on a range of prescribed factors, and determining their relevance to an individual's offending behavior (Hart, Douglas, & Guy, 2016). The practitioner judges the presence and severity of a range of predetermined risk factors and comes to a final judgment concerning risk level (i.e., low, medium, or high). SPJ assessments are geared towards managing risk and they often involve the development of risk scenarios (Hart et al., 2016). It is important to note that due to its idiographic nature and dependence on practitioner judgment, SPJ assessment is more reliant on theories of offending to guide decisions about the presence, severity, and relevance of particular features (i.e., linking them with offending). However, it may be argued that any risk assessment method which relies on practitioner judgment (including some actuarial tools) must be based in some underpinning theory of offending (Ward, 2019). For this reason, while it is not our primary concern, the implications of the analysis contained in this book may extend to the prediction of risk, in addition to informing the management of risk and treatment. The role of explanation becomes increasingly important when the aims of prediction are extended from merely producing a numerical estimate of risk (i.e., beyond the second generation).

A wide range of risk assessment tools have been developed to ensure that risk assessment is as objective and reliable as possible, and that it is suitable for the purpose it was designed for (Cording & Beggs Christofferson, 2017). These tools vary in their focus on static or dynamic factors or both, stable and acute dynamic factors, and some even include scales containing protective factors or strengths (i.e., risk reducing factors; Heffernan & Ward, 2017). They also differ in their purpose within forensic practice (e.g., managing and responding to changes in risk, treatment allocation and planning, and measuring post-treatment changes), and the kind of offending they are designed to predict (e.g., violent, sexual, and/or general offending). Risk measures are developed via statistical and psychometric techniques which bring together numerous personal and contextual features statistically associated with recidivism. These scales are additive, and it is suggested that they include only items which increase predictive accuracy, cover multiple domains of risk, include static and dynamic predictors, and that their use extends to informing the risk and need principles (Cording & Beggs Christofferson, 2017). The most commonly used risk assessment measures have been shown to predict recidivism at a level better than chance, this is the basis of the risk principle. However, there are concerns about construct validity and some researchers have highlighted the need for more theoretically driven research to inform practice (Cording, Beggs Christofferson, & Grace, 2016; Kroner, Mills, & Reddon, 2005).

1.3 Treatment

As above, and in line with the need principle of the RNR, the second role of DRF in forensic practice is informing interventions by identifying targets for change. The rationale for providing correctional treatment is a belief that the causes of crime can be ameliorated, programs aim to do this by targeting DRF and building skills which can overcome these deficits (e.g., communication, emotion regulation, cognitive restructuring). The only reason for targeting these factors to reduce crime is the belief in a causal link with future offending behavior (Ward & Beech, 2015). In the realm of treatment, DRF play a role in both case formulation (i.e., an individually tailored explanation of a person's offending and its causes) and program design and delivery. Because they are linked with offending at the aggregate level, they are a logical starting point when designing interventions for large groups of individuals; they represent a common set of problems. The assumption is then that the DRF identified in risk research are also implicated in individuals' offending, they are incorporated into case formulation and inform an individual's treatment goals. They are then the focus of treatment and any progress is measured against these, for example, whether the individual has demonstrated shifts towards more prosocial attitudes or developed ways to manage antisocial influences. This is viewed as a reduction in risk, perhaps accompanied by more awareness of their high-risk situations and DRF (i.e., relapse prevention plans). The logic of this focus on DRF throughout treatment depends on their causal relationship with offending.

The field of correctional psychology has become increasingly interested in factors that *decrease* the probability of reoffending, what have been termed protective factors (PF; Heffernan & Ward, 2017). This makes sense considering that the goal of correctional practice is to reduce the likelihood that following punishment and/or treatment individuals will harm others. de Vries Robbé, Mann, Maruna, and Thornton (2015) define a PF as "a feature of a person that lowers the risk of reoffending" (p. 18) and propose that "the definition of a protective factor should encompass social, interpersonal, and environmental factors as well as psychological and behavioral features" (p. 18). Because our focus is on DRF in this book we will only refer to PF within this context and not comment on them in any detail (for detailed discussion and analyses of PF see Heffernan & Ward, 2017; Ward, 2017).

1.4 Explanation

In addition to functioning as predictors and treatment targets, DRF are the foundation of numerous theories of offending and risk (Bonta & Andrews, 2017; Mann et al., 2010). They are central to explanations of offending. This includes single-factor and multifactorial theories, and theories depicting the offence process (Ward & Hudson, 1998a). For example, there are numerous theories of cognitive distortions or attitudes supportive of offending and these are included, alongside problems with self-regulation, relationships, and sexual functioning, within multifactorial theories of sexual offending. In this sense DRF guide practice but they also guide research; they are the focus of both theory development and empirical studies (i.e., testing their predictive utility and measuring change). In the following chapter we offer a brief summary of the empirical research concerning the measurement of DRF, their predictive validity, and the extent to which they change over time. The current chapter will highlight the centrality of DRF in theories of offending and thus the strength of the assumption that they play a causal role in offending. The focus of these theories ranges from general explanations of criminal conduct (e.g., the PCC) and risk factors, to more specific offending behaviors. The specific theories we will outline here are from the sexual offending field, although comparable theories exist to explain the occurrence of violence and other types of offending.

First, it is important to note that rehabilitation frameworks are underpinned by general theories of offending. They contain over-arching values (e.g., harm reduction), principles and guidelines (e.g., the RNR principles), and assumptions about the causes of offending, which rely upon various theories of crime and offending behavior (Ward, 2019; Ward, Melser, & Yates, 2007). For example, the RNR model is grounded in a *general personality and cognitive social learning* (GPCSL) theory of criminal conduct. This perspective brings together empirical research (i.e., meta-analyses and prediction) and theoretical work to inform practice within the criminal justice system. It is built upon criminological and psychological theories, and, as the name suggests, views social learning and reinforcement as particularly important in the initiation and maintenance of criminal conduct. The central eight criminogenic needs are thought to influence the cognitive decision to commit a crime within any given situation (Bonta & Andrews, 2017), they play a causal role. For example, the presence of multiple risk factors (e.g., antisocial attitudes, offence-supportive associates, antisocial personality) increases the likelihood that an individual will commit an offence. The GPCSL approach acknowledges a range of bio-psycho-social influences upon the development of criminogenic needs and criminal behavior, for example, family of origin, neighborhood features, temperament, gender, age, ethnicity, and so on.

To explain the relationship between different types of risk factor and their functions in influencing behavior, Beech and Ward (2004) developed an *etiological model of risk*. According to the etiological model, stable DRF are psychological dispositions which indicate a vulnerability to commit an offence, while static factors, such as criminal history, are evidence of these traits manifesting in the past. Acute DRF arise when vulnerabilities are triggered (e.g., by peers, conflict, substance use) resulting in internal states (e.g., distress, intoxication) which lead to an offence. As noted earlier, this distinction between traits and states is compatible with a propensities model of risk and the idea that psychologically meaningful risk factors or vulnerabilities may or may not lead to an offence in any situation (Mann et al., 2010). This model aimed to bridge the gap between empirical and theoretical research by attempting to explain how these predictors may over time be causally related to risk. It offers a useful way to understand the overlap between different types of risk factor (i.e., intersectionality), but does not possess adequate detail to explain how risk factors interact to cause crime.

In comparison to these general models of crime and risk factors, theories of offending depict more specific behaviors. These are most often based upon correlational analyses of the phenomena associated with offending (i.e., DRF); they are driven by 'ground level' data (Cording et al., 2016). While this makes sense as we want to be able to describe the functional relationships between variables, it is also problematic because correlation does not indicate causation in any straightforward sense. There are typically three levels of theory identified in the field of forensic and correctional psychology, each dedicated to explaining different targets (Ward & Hudson, 1998a). The first level consists of multi-factorial theories that combine several factors or domains thought to influence offending behavior. For example, Marshall and Barbaree's (1990) *integrated theory* and Ward and Siegert's (2002) *pathways model* are both intended to explain sexual offending, and encompass self-regulation, cognitive, affective, interpersonal, and sexual domains of risk. The second level of theory is concerned with explaining single factors and focuses in depth on specific categories or domains of risk, such as offence-related attitudes or relationship difficulties. There is no attempt to explain why a particular type of crime occurs (e.g., sexual offending), rather the emphasis is on accounting for the presence of specific factors associated with offending (e.g., empathy deficits linked to sexual offending). The third level is dedicated to descriptions of the offence and relapse process, such as Ward and Hudson's (1998b) *self-regulation model*, and Finkelhor's (1984) *pre-conditions* model of sexual offending.

1.5 Theories of Sexual Offending

To illustrate the scope of theories of offending and their reliance on DRF, we will now briefly outline five influential theories of sexual offending, as well as providing a brief critique of each. We will then introduce a number of recent developments which emerged based on the concern that DRF were leading the field into a "theoretical dead-end" (Ward & Beech, 2015).

Finkelhor (1984) proposed four *preconditions* which must be satisfied for a sexual offence to occur. The first is a motivator which predisposes an individual to engage in an offence. This can be one of three risk factors: emotional congruence with children, sexual attraction to children, or blockage of appropriate means to achieve sexual needs (Finkelhor, 1984). The second precondition is overcoming internal inhibitions, for example by rationalizing and justifying behavior or using substances to temporarily suspend judgment concerning the rightness or wrongness of behavior. The third is overcoming external barriers such as gaining unsupervised access to a potential victim, and the fourth involves overcoming any resistance from the victim. This theory proposes that the first two preconditions are internal causes and the final two explain how a motivated individual engages with other people and their environment to facilitate an offence. While Finkelhor's (1984) preconditions integrate a number of observable features of sexual offences or individuals who have committed these (e.g., DRF such as cognitive distortions, self-regulation problems, emotional congruence, sexual deviance) and accounts for different motivations (e.g., sexual needs, intimacy), this lacks depth and clarity. For example, it is unclear what exactly is involved in emotional congruence, blockage, or rationalization. In order to explain how an individual becomes motivated and then overcomes internal inhibitions theorists must refer to psychological processes and mechanisms.

Marshall and Barbaree's (1990) *integrated theory* incorporated both distal and proximal influences on the development of sexual offending. This theory sees childhood adversity causing the development of problems associated with sexual offending (i.e., DRF) through biological development and social learning. These problems then persist and result in the development of additional risk factors, for example, problems with interpersonal functioning leading to social rejection and loneliness in adolescence. In contexts where there is opportunity (e.g., unsupervised access to children) these vulnerabilities can lead to a sexual offence. The reinforcing nature of the offence and post-hoc rationalizations and justifications for behavior maintain offending over time. While this theory represents substantial progress in the field, due to its broad nature it is overly vague and lacks depth. It can account for the development and maintenance of problematic sexual behavior over time at a general level but cannot explain how these vulnerabilities may cause an offence at any time.

Hall and Hirschman's (1992) *quadripartite theory* combined cognitive distortions, affective dyscontrol, sexual arousal, and personality problems. Personality problems are seen as enduring vulnerabilities, while the other three factors depend on both internal and external states. The quadripartite theory proposes that one of these four factors functions as a 'primary motivator', while all four are likely implicated in an offence. The primary motivator is the strongest of the four risk factors in any given instance and acts to "push" the individual over the threshold necessary to commit an offence. The reliance on one factor as driving the offending is somewhat limited, but it does allow for the categorization of individuals according to their primary motivator. For example, those who are driven by sexual motives versus those who offend to cope with emotional problems. This may be useful in terms of identifying general problem areas to target in intervention, however it lacks clarity in terms of the interaction between the four types of risk factor. In addition, the reliance on 'personality problems' as a catch all category for personal vulnerabilities is vague.

Ward and Siegert's (2002) *pathways model* built upon these existing theories and hypothesizes that four mechanisms collectively cause a sexual offence: intimacy and social deficits, distorted sexual scripts, cognitive distortions, and a lack of emotion-regulation skills. These authors also propose that a primary mechanism drives behavior, but that all four domains are implicated in offending. For example, distorted (i.e., pedophilic) sexual scripts may lead to sexual offending when an individual is experiencing rejection from peers and is able to either justify or suspend judgment of the behavior. This model represents progress as it acknowledges the heterogeneity of pathways to sexual offending and the interaction between DRF, but it is lacking in the sense that it still does not explain precisely *how* they interact to lead to an offence.

The final theory we will mention here is Ward and Beech's (2006) *integrated theory of sexual offending* (ITSO). The ITSO widened the scope of etiological theories by incorporating biological and neurological influences on offending. It includes the four domains of risk discussed above and aims to increase understanding of their interaction through the concept of "interlocking neuropsychological functions" (Ward & Beech, 2006). These interactions occur between three core psychological systems; motivational and emotional, perception and memory, and action selection and control, and they cause the problems which lead to sexual offending (i.e., DRF). The ITSO is novel in its combination of developmental and evolutionary perspectives with proximal influences such as neurological mechanisms and contextual features. Unfortunately, due to its wide scope it is limited in its detail on any one aspect of the theory. In addition, it overlooks the first-person experiential level of understanding, meaning that it does not adequately account for human agency and self-determination. This is a shortcoming which more recent theories have aimed to address.

1.6 Recent Theoretical Developments: Agency

The theories discussed above are centered upon combinations of empirically supported DRF for sexual offending; they combine problems such as sexual deviance, cognitive distortions, interpersonal difficulties, and poor self-regulation. They aim to explain how these problems can lead to sexual offending, but they tend to overlook critical sources of motivation and agency, and overall lack depth in being able to explain why persons have the problems exhibited and how exactly they lead to offending for some individuals but not others. We believe that due to their focus on DRF and specific outcomes (i.e., illegal sexual behavior) they have inadvertently ignored important determinants of behavior. They are incomplete explanations because they focus on negative outcomes and correlates but do not include normative or adaptive aspects of human functioning, those psychological mechanisms which influence behavior more generally. For example, motivation, values, attributions, expectations, and so on.

More recently authors have begun to develop theories which conceptualize DRF in a different way. It has been suggested that DRF are "symptom-like" aspects of persons which often co-occur with criminal behavior but do not cause it (Ward & Beech, 2015; Ward & Fortune, 2016). A number of recent theories have drawn from the concept of *agency* and developed explanations of offending as a form of goal-directed behavior. From this perspective behavior is motivated by particular needs or desires, and then a set of psychological mechanisms or capacities (e.g., attention, memory, control, schemas) allows individuals to engage with their environment in goal-directed action. When applying this perspective to criminal behavior, DRF are aspects of persons *and* their environments which *indicate* a higher probability that these goal-directed actions will involve crime. For example, obstacles which get in the way of goal-directed behavior (i.e., problems with self-regulation, control, problem-solving, substance use, environmental constraints) or aspects of a person's behaviors and environments which indicate a pattern of criminal engagement (i.e., associates, violence, attitudes toward crime). Thus, DRF are symptom-like features which can be measured to estimate risk but cannot themselves be causal (although they may reflect the manifestation of underlying causal mechanisms). We will now outline five recent theoretical perspectives on DRF which rely on the concept of agency, several of these incorporate protective factors or strengths.

The *agency model of risk* (AMR; Heffernan & Ward, 2015) is a dynamic, interactional model which depicts the relationship between an agent (i.e., an individual capable of forming plans and acting intentionally) and their context, and proposes that both play a part in facilitating behavior. The agent is comprised of three 'levels' which give rise to the development of goals and action sequences. These levels are biological systems, social roles, and personal identity. Depending on contextual triggers and internal motivators (i.e., unmet needs) one or more of these levels may influence the development of a goal. For example, a teacher (social role) who views himself as vulnerable and misunderstood (identity) and is experiencing rejection (social context) and loneliness (i.e., interpersonal needs unmet) may form the goal of sexual intimacy in general, or perhaps because attempts with women have previously failed the goal is specifically sexual intimacy with a child (i.e., a student). Due to his unsupervised access to children (physical and social context) and his understanding that sexual contact with minors is illegal and subject to punishment (normative context), he carefully selects a vulnerable child and identifies strategies likely to gain their trust, thereby minimizing the chances of detection. He then implements these plans and monitors their success, altering his strategies and goals where necessary in response to his context. The AMR represents a shift in focus to the capacities and processes underpinning agency, but it lacks depth in that it does not unpack the role of cognition and emotion across action sequences.

Thornton (2016) developed a theory of DRF based on the *good lives model* (GLM; Ward & Maruna, 2007), *schema modes* (Beck, 1996), and the *theory of reasoned action* (TRA; Fishbein & Ajzen, 2010). He argues that the dominant view of DRF as offence supportive propensities neglects human agency and so fails to focus on the causes of criminal behavior. The GLM is utilised as a framework to understand sources of motivation (i.e., fundamental human interests or primary human goods); essentially answering the question: what is it that people seek? The second element of this theory involves goal-directed decision-making; how do people guide their behavior to meet these interests? The TRA offers an account of reasoning based on outcome expectancies, social pressure, and self-efficacy. Essentially the attractiveness of behavior, how others are likely to judge it, and how successful one expects to be in enacting a behavior. Schemas are involved as an intermediate zone between goals and reasoned action, containing representations of environmental features such as people, places, and situations (e.g., scripts and strategies). These representations allow individuals to weigh up the potential success and attractiveness of various types of action, and they can be adaptive or maladaptive in nature.

In applying this same theory to desistance processes and items from the *Structured Assessment of PROtective Factors for violence risk* tool (SAPROF; de Vogel, de Ruiter, Bouman, & de Vries Robbé, 2009; de Vogel, de Vries Robbé, de Ruiter, & Bouman, 2011), Thornton, Kelley, and Nelligan (2017) developed a theory of protective factors (PF). At an abstract level, Thornton et al. (2017) propose that PF can be understood within a broader context of DRF; the two categories are viewed as "families of related concepts" (p. 30). It makes sense that Thornton's (2016) theory of DRF applies also to PF, and that goal-directed processes that lead an individual towards prosocial behavior rather than offending are linked with PF. At an intermediate level, Thornton et al. (2017) propose that many PF may be conceptualized as arenas within which certain protective processes occur (e.g., employment, relationships). Finally, they state that PF will take different forms and operate in different arenas depending on various characteristics of persons and their specific concerns. Four PF categories are proposed in the theory: *dynamic internal*, *social*, *professionally provided*, and *openness* to *professionally provided PF*. The examples used (i.e., SAPROF items; de Vogel et al., 2009) are a mixture of internal abilities and characteristics, and the arenas within which they operate. For example, dynamic internal factors (e.g., empathy, coping skills, and self-control) may facilitate engagement with social contexts (e.g., work, leisure, relationships) and openness to professionally provided factors such as supervision and treatment. These examples mirror internal and external risk domains, and in this sense can point to surface-level aspects of internal and external desistance processes (instead of offending), but do not offer a more in-depth theoretical account of how PF reduce risk. Despite this limitation, the idea that DRF and PF are category labels for two groups of inversely related characteristics and the arenas that they manifest within is a simple but attractive one, as there has long been confusion regarding the theoretical relationship between risk and PF.

Durrant (2017) presents an evolutionary perspective on DRF and PF, based upon individual differences and environmental conditions. His framework contains two models outlining how and why developmental PF reduce the likelihood of future criminal behavior (Durrant, 2017). The first is based on the evolutionary theory of *life history strategies* (Belsky, Schlomer, & Ellis, 2012) which vary in their pace depending on individual and environmental features. For example, a fast life history strategy typically develops when an individual is exposed to environments which are dangerous and unpredictable, as this is adaptive in terms of reproduction and survival. In contrast, a slow life history strategy develops when an individual exists within safer or more predictable environments, as there is less need to protect the self and others from threat; the individual engages in long-term thinking, as there is no reason to speed up the reproduction process. From an evolutionary perspective, the point of an adaptation is to increase an individual's chances of surviving in order to pass on copies of his or her genes to future generations. If organisms evaluate their life situation as risky then it makes sense from a strictly biological viewpoint to engage in reproduction at an earlier age before they suffer injury or even death. A faster strategy is associated with greater risk taking, violence, and reckless or impulsive behavior, while a slower strategy is associated with a more balanced lifestyle and well thought out plans. It should come as no surprise that Durrant (2017) links slower life history strategies with developmental PF, and faster life history strategies with DRF. This makes sense from an evolutionary perspective, and suggests that perhaps offending, DRF, and related behaviors can be considered adaptive in some contexts; that is to say that they can be useful in self-preservation, reproduction, and survival—at least in the short term.

Durrant's (2017) second model is based on the evolutionary concept of *plasticity*, or differences in an individual's susceptibility to environmental conditions. Unpacking the concept of plasticity, Durrant (2017) states that individuals are able to:

> …reliably adjust their behaviour in response to enduring features of the environment. However, there is also a widespread recognition among evolutionary biologists that there are also significant individual differences in plasticity that reflect the outcome of selective processes. In other words, individuals vary in the extent that their behaviour is plastic in response to features of the developing environment. (p. 8)

He proposes that whether a developmental feature is a DRF or PF (i.e., functions to increase or decrease risk) depends upon how easily the individual is influenced by their environment. In this sense, PF are positive environmental features *and* their influence on the individual. For example, a stable home environment may be protective, but individuals will differ in their sensitivity to this developmental PF (or opposite DRF). It has been suggested that those who are more easily influenced by contexts may be more sensitive to both positive (PF) and negative (DRF) conditions, and vice versa. However, in some cases individuals may be more or less sensitive to PF than DRF. Thus, plasticity may offer some explanation as to why some individuals with risk factors do not offend, and also why certain people may be less responsive to positive external influences (e.g., social control, professional support). Durrant (2017) concludes that "before we can make theoretical progress in understanding antisocial behaviour … and the factors that predict those individual differences (risk and protective), we need to have a general understanding of – for want of a better term – our 'human nature'" (p. 6), and that "in order to understand antisocial behaviour we need to locate such acts within the broader context of normative human development" (p. 6). These suggestions are in line with our aim to provide a framework which can generate and guide future theoretical work, and ultimately inform more effective forensic practice.

Serin, Chadwick, and Lloyd's (2016) *agency filter model* is another recent attempt at providing an explanation of the relationship between DRF and PF and offending. It was developed in response to the confusion surrounding what PF are and how they might ameliorate risk. This model proposes that DRF and PF exert their influence upon behavior via a filter containing "agency, self-identification, hope, optimism, self-efficacy, attributions, social supports" (Serin et al., 2016, p. 164). This filter represents the agent's interpretation of events and situations which could be risky or protective; essentially how they respond to (mainly contextual) PF and DRF. For example, whether attaining employment is meaningful enough to direct a person away from offending. The idea of an individualized filter can begin to explain why the same factors may influence individuals differently, and how other 'non-criminogenic' factors such as identity and self-efficacy may influence risk of recidivism. It brings agency and self-determination into the equation but arguably lacks depth in terms of explaining how these factors might interact to cause behavior. In addition, it seems that DRF and PF in this model mainly consist of external events and situations or internal states which the agent responds to. It pays less attention to an individual's capacities and does not account for the role of dysfunctional psychological mechanisms (e.g., impaired self-control) in some instances of offending.

The *predictive agency model* (PAM; Heffernan & Ward, 2017) is based on the assumption that human beings are forward-looking and motivated to attain certain outcomes that they anticipate will benefit them and/or avoid harmful consequences (see Fig. 1.1). It views the mind as *a predictive engine* and emotion as critical in generating and evaluating predictions. According to the PAM predictions are based on an individual's general causal models, or mental representations of the self, others, and the environment—including sources of risk and reward. The PAM proposes that in specific situations these general models are used to generate situation specific local models (i.e., of the current situation, people present, sources of risk/reward). The theory of reasoned action (TRA; Fishbein & Ajzen, 2010) is then used to explain decision-making (although this process may be more or less conscious and deliberate). For example, specific local models are used to evaluate different possible actions; predict their success, likely reactions from others, and the probability of reward associated with potential actions (i.e., offending). After an action is selected and performed, the individual experiences the outcomes (i.e., success,

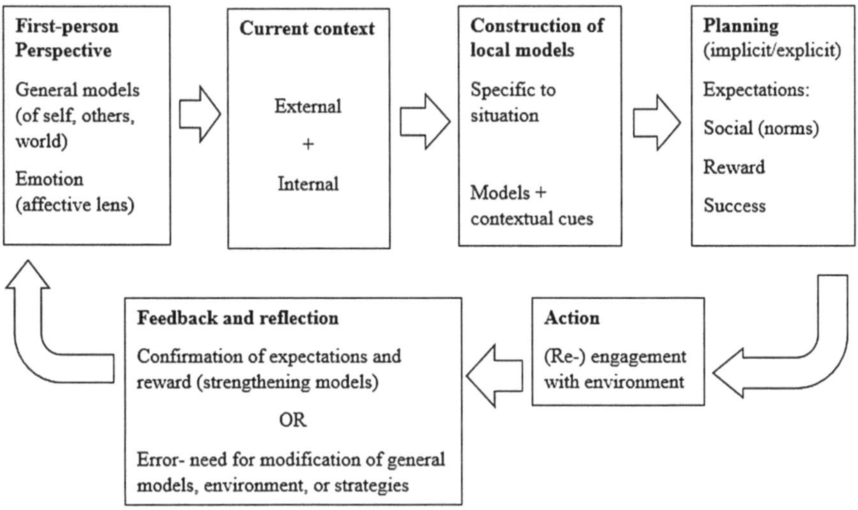

Fig. 1.1 The predictive agency model. Reprinted from "A Comprehensive Theory of Dynamic Risk and Protective Factors," by R. Heffernan and T. Ward, 2017, *Aggression and Violent Behavior, 37*, p. 137. Copyright 2017 by Elsevier Ltd. Reprinted with permission

responses from others, emotional response/reward) and this feeds back into general models, either strengthening them if the outcome was in line with the prediction or potentially weakening or adjusting them if the predicted outcome did not occur. The PAM is useful in providing a psychological level explanation of the capacities which contribute to the generation of predictions and decisions concerning possible actions. However, it lacks depth when it comes to the sub-personal and socio-cultural mechanisms underpinning behavior, for this reason the PAM will be utilized later in our framework for reformulating DRF.

1.7 Causal Mechanisms

Encouraging and guiding the current emphasis on agency is the need for *causal explanations* of offending which depict underlying psychological *mechanisms* to be targeted in treatment. This will be explored further in the following chapter, where we develop the argument that the causal status of DRF is currently uncertain and therefore their foundational place in theories of offending is misguided. There are those who would argue that because correctional interventions "work", it does not matter whether DRF are causes or not. However, we suggest that although there are interventions which have demonstrated some success in reducing recidivism, there are many which have not and, overall, the positive effects are moderate and variable across studies (Heffernan, Wegerhoff, & Ward, 2019; Hough, 2010). For example, a meta-analysis by Gannon, Olver, Mallion, and James (2019) found that "relative reductions in offense specific recidivism were 32.6% for sexual offense programs, 36.0% for domestic violence programs, and 24.3% for general violence programs" (p. 1). In contrast, a meta-analysis by Jolliffe and Farrington (2007) found an eight to 11% difference in general recidivism and seven to eight percent difference in violent recidivism between treated and untreated groups, with higher quality studies finding weaker effects. In terms of sexual offending, Schmucker and Lösel's (2015) international meta-analysis found recidivism rates of 10.1% for those who completed treatment, compared to 13.7% for those who did not receive treatment (representing a relative reduction of 26.3%). Further, researchers have struggled to identify significant changes to DRF throughout and after treatment (Cording et al., 2016; Heffernan, Wegerhoff, & Ward, 2019). Finally, as in medicine, mechanistic explanations have the potential to provide greater awareness of possible intervention targets (Thagard, 1999). These points provide support for the scientific and practical value of constructing richer conceptualizations of DRF and clarifying their role in explanations of offending.

In an analysis of the state of research into what works to reduce reoffending, Hough (2010) observes that:

> there has been over-investment (both financially and intellectually) in a technocratic model of reducing reoffending that attaches too much importance in accredited programmes and packages, and under-investment in models that see the process of 'people changing' as a

> complex social skill. The technocratic model seriously underestimates this complexity, and its advocates wrongly assumes that experimental research can readily identify the causal processes at work in helping people stop offending. (p. 12)

This quote highlights the preoccupation with providing tools for prediction and rules for "success" in intervention design and delivery. While this is an admirable goal, unfortunately it has come at the expense of developing rich explanations for human behavior and applying these to the populations of interest. Mechanistic explanations are essential in explaining and altering criminal behavior.

1.8 Summary

To conclude this chapter, DRF are changeable aspects of persons and their environments which are statistically associated with recidivism. They are used in practice both to predict and reduce the likelihood of further offending. We suggest that while the first role of DRF (as predictors) is justified, their transportation into the realm of treatment relies on the assumption that they have a causal relationship with offending; this relationship has not been proven. This approach represents a conflation of the related, but distinct, tasks of prediction and explanation. Interventions rely on explanations of offending to guide practitioners' understanding of how these factors cause crime and thus why they are problematic for individuals. Historically explanations of offending have relied on DRF as causes, the belief in this relationship is so strong that it is rarely questioned. As is the belief that changing these factors is the key to reducing recidivism.

We suggest that within forensic and correctional practice DRF are best viewed as predictive constructs that are generally effective in assigning probabilities to individuals based on group membership (e.g., risk bands such as low, medium, or high), but on their own are unable to tell us what might influence individual risk. We argue that at present the relationship between predictors and causes (i.e., treatment targets) is unclear, and that the role of DRF in treatment depends on their ability to explain why individuals offend and what might facilitate desistance. In our view DRF are best viewed as boundary riders; they tell us that there are a number of possible problems operating within a particular domain such as crime supportive beliefs, contextual features, mental states, social situations, and psychological dispositions. But they do not tell us what the specific problems are. For that we need to enlist explanatory theories and move beyond "one size fits all" approaches to assessment and treatment. The next chapter will expand upon this argument by providing a critical analysis of DRF, including both conceptual and empirical problems. The following chapters will offer some preliminary suggestions to move the field on from the theoretical dead end which will inevitably result from a narrow focus on DRF as causal explanations for offending.

References

Andrews, D. A., & Bonta, J. (2010). *The psychology of criminal conduct* (5th ed.). New Providence, NJ: LexisNexis.

Andrews, D. A., Bonta, J., & Wormith, S. J. (2010). The level of service (LS) assessment of adults and older adolescents. In R. K. Otto & K. Douglas (Eds.), *Handbook of violence risk assessment* (pp. 199–225). New York, NY: Routledge.

Beck, A. T. (1996). Beyond belief: A theory of modes, personality, and psychopathology. In P. Salkovskis (Ed.), *Frontiers of cognitive therapy* (pp. 1–25). New York, NY: Guilford.

Beech, A. R., & Craig, L. A. (2012). The current status of static and dynamic factors in sexual offender risk assessment. *Journal of Aggression, Conflict and Peace Research, 4*(4), 169–118. https://doi.org/10.1108/17596591211270671

Beech, A. R., & Ward, T. (2004). The integration of etiology and risk in sexual offenders: A theoretical framework. *Aggression and Violent Behavior, 10*(1), 31–63. https://doi.org/10.1016/j.avb.2003.08.002

Belsky, J., Schlomer, G. L., & Ellis, B. (2012). Beyond cumulative risk: Distinguishing harshness and unpredictability as determinants of parenting and early life history strategy. *Developmental Psychology, 48*, 662–673. https://doi.org/10.1037/a004454

Bonta, J., & Andrews, D. A. (2017). *The psychology of criminal conduct* (6th ed.). New York, NY: Routledge.

Cording, J. R., & Beggs Christofferson, S. M. (2017). Theoretical and practical issues for the measurement of protective factors. *Aggression and Violent Behavior, 32*, 45–54. https://doi.org/10.1016/j.avb.2016.12.007

Cording, J. R., Beggs Christofferson, S. M., & Grace, R. C. (2016). Challenges for the theory and application of dynamic risk factors. *Psychology, Crime & Law, 22*(1–2), 84–103. https://doi.org/10.1080/1068316x.2015.1111367

de Vogel, V., de Ruiter, C., Bouman, Y., & de Vries Robbé, M. (2009). *SAPROF. Guidelines for the assessment of protective factors for violence risk. English version.* Utrecht, The Netherlands: Forum Educatief.

de Vogel, V., de Vries Robbé, M., de Ruiter, C., & Bouman, Y. H. (2011). Assessing protective factors in forensic psychiatric practice: Introducing the SAPROF. *International Journal of Forensic Mental Health, 10*(3), 171–177. https://doi.org/10.1080/14999013.2011.600230

de Vries Robbé, M., Mann, R. E., Maruna, S., & Thornton, D. (2015). An exploration of protective factors supporting desistance from sexual offending. *Sexual Abuse, 27*(1), 16–33. https://doi.org/10.1177/1079063214547582

Durrant, R. (2017). Why do protective factors protect? An evolutionary developmental perspective. *Aggression and Violent Behavior, 32*, 4–10. https://doi.org/10.1016/j.avb.2016.12.002

Finkelhor, D. (1984). *Child sexual abuse: New theory and research.* New York, NY: The Free Press.

Fishbein, M., & Ajzen, I. (2010). *Predicting and changing behavior: The reasoned action approach.* New York, NY: Psychology Press (Taylor & Francis).

Gannon, T. A., Olver, M. E., Mallion, J. S., & James, M. (2019). Does specialized psychological treatment for offending reduce recidivism? A meta-analysis examining staff and program variables as predictors of treatment effectiveness. *Clinical Psychology Review, 73*, 101752. https://doi.org/10.1016/j.cpr.2019.101752

Hall, G. C. N., & Hirschman, R. (1992). Sexual aggression against children: A conceptual perspective of etiology. *Criminal Justice and Behavior, 19*(1), 8–23. https://doi.org/10.1177/0093854892019001003

Hanson, R. K., & Harris, A. J. (2000). Where should we intervene? Dynamic predictors of sexual offense recidivism. *Criminal Justice and Behavior, 27*(1), 6–35. https://doi.org/10.1177/0093854800027001002

Hanson, R. K., & Morton-Bourgon, K. E. (2009). The accuracy of recidivism risk assessments for sexual offenders: A meta-analysis of 118 prediction studies. *Psychological Assessment, 21*, 1–21. https://doi.org/10.1037/a0014421

Hart, S. D. (2009). Evidence-based assessment of risk for sexual violence. *Chapman Journal of Criminal Justice, 1*, 143–165.

Hart, S. D., Douglas, K. S., & Guy, L. S. (2016). The structured professional judgement approach to violence risk assessment: Origins, nature, and advances. In *The Wiley handbook on the theories, assessment and treatment of sexual offending* (pp. 643–666). Hoboken, NJ: Wiley.

Hart, S. D., & Logan, C. (2011). Formulation of violent risk using evidence-based assessments: The structured professional judgment approach. In P. Sturmey & M. McMurran (Eds.), *Forensic case formulation* (pp. 3–32). West Sussex, UK: Wiley.

Heffernan, R., & Ward, T. (2015). The conceptualization of dynamic risk factors in child sex offenders: An agency model. *Aggression and Violent Behavior, 24*, 250–260. https://doi.org/10.1016/j.avb.2015.07.001

Heffernan, R., & Ward, T. (2017). A comprehensive theory of dynamic risk and protective factors. *Aggression and Violent Behavior, 37*, 129–141. https://doi.org/10.1016/j.avb.2017.10.003

Heffernan, R., Wegerhoff, D., & Ward, T. (2019). Dynamic risk factors: Conceptualization, measurement, and evidence. *Aggression and Violent Behavior, 48*, 6–16. https://doi.org/10.1016/j.avb.2019.06.004

Hough, M. (2010). Gold standard or fool's gold? The pursuit of certainty in experimental criminology. *Criminology & Criminal Justice, 10*(1), 11–22. https://doi.org/10.1177/1748895809352597

Jolliffe, D., & Farrington, D. P. (2007). *A systematic review of the national and international evidence on the effectiveness of interventions with violent offenders* (Series 16/07). London, UK: Ministry of Justice Research.

Kroner, D. G., Mills, J. F., & Reddon, J. R. (2005). A coffee can, factor analysis, and prediction of antisocial behavior: The structure of criminal risk. *International Journal of Law and Psychiatry, 28*(4), 360–374. https://doi.org/10.1016/j.ijlp.2004.01.011

Lovins, B. K., Latessa, E. J., May, T., & Lux, J. (2018). Validating the Ohio risk assessment system community supervision tool with a diverse sample from Texas. *Corrections, 3*(3), 186–202. https://doi.org/10.1080/23774657.2017.1361798

Mann, R. E., Hanson, R. K., & Thornton, D. (2010). Assessing risk for sexual recidivism: Some proposals on the nature of psychologically meaningful risk factors. *Sexual Abuse, 22*(2), 191–217. https://doi.org/10.1177/1079063210366039

Marshall, W. L., & Barbaree, H. E. (1990). *An integrated theory of sexual offending*. New York, NY: Springer.

Olver, M. E., & Wong, S. C. (2019). Offender risk and need assessment: Theory, research, and applications. In *The Wiley international handbook of correctional psychology* (pp. 461–475). Hoboken, NJ: Wiley.

Schmucker, M., & Lösel, F. (2015). The effects of sexual offender treatment on recidivism: An international meta-analysis of sound quality evaluations. *Journal of Experimental Criminology, 11*(4), 597–630. https://doi.org/10.1007/s11292-015-9241-z

Serin, R. C., Chadwick, N., & Lloyd, C. D. (2016). Dynamic risk and protective factors. *Psychology, Crime & Law, 22*(1–2), 151–170. https://doi.org/10.1080/1068316X.2015.1112013

Thagard, P. (1999). *How scientists explain disease*. Princeton, NJ: Princeton University Press.

Thornton, D. (2016). Developing a theory of dynamic risk. *Psychology, Crime & Law, 22*(1–2), 138–150. https://doi.org/10.1080/1068316x.2015.1109092

Thornton, D., Kelley, S. M., & Nelligan, K. E. (2017). Protective factors and mental illness in men with a history of sexual offending. *Aggression and Violent Behavior, 32*, 29–36. https://doi.org/10.1016/j.avb.2016.12.003

Ward, T. (2017). Prediction and agency: The role of protective factors in correctional rehabilitation and desistance. *Aggression and Violent Behavior, 32*, 19–28. https://doi.org/10.1016/j.avb.2016.11.012

Ward, T. (2019). Why theory matters in correctional psychology. *Aggression and Violent Behavior, 48*, 36–45. https://doi.org/10.1016/j.avb.2019.08.015
Ward, T., & Beech, A. R. (2006). An integrated theory of sexual offending. *Aggression and Violent Behavior, 11*, 44–63. https://doi.org/10.1016/j.avb.2005.05.002
Ward, T., & Beech, A. R. (2015). Dynamic risk factors: A theoretical dead-end? *Psychology. Crime & Law, 21*(2), 100–113. https://doi.org/10.1080/1068316x.2014.917854
Ward, T., & Fortune, C.-A. (2016). The role of dynamic risk factors in the explanation of offending. *Aggression and Violent Behavior, 29*, 79–88. https://doi.org/10.1016/j.avb.2016.06.007
Ward, T., & Hudson, S. M. (1998a). The construction and development of theory in the sexual offending area: A metatheoretical framework. *Sexual Abuse: A Journal of Research and Treatment, 10*(1), 47–63. https://doi.org/10.1177/107906329801000106
Ward, T., & Hudson, S. M. (1998b). A model of the relapse process in sexual offenders. *Journal of Interpersonal Violence, 13*, 700–725. https://doi.org/10.1177/088626098013006003
Ward, T., & Maruna, S. (2007). *Rehabilitation: Beyond the risk paradigm*. London, UK: Routledge.
Ward, T., Melser, J., & Yates, P. M. (2007). Reconstructing the risk-need-responsivity model: A theoretical elaboration and evaluation. *Aggression and Violent Behavior, 12*(2), 208–228. https://doi.org/10.1016/j.avb.2006.07.001
Ward, T., & Siegert, R. J. (2002). Toward a comprehensive theory of child sexual abuse: A theory knitting perspective. *Psychology, Crime & Law, 8*(4), 319–351. https://doi.org/10.1080/10683160208401823

Chapter 2
Critical Analysis of Dynamic Risk Factors

Abstract The assumption that dynamic risk factors (DRF) are causal concepts as well as predictive ones is apparent in their dual roles in practice and in the theories explored in the previous chapter; an assumption that we argue is mistaken. In this chapter we examine a number of conceptual and empirical problems with DRF which we view as arising from their composite nature. Specifically, the conceptual problems of incoherence, lack of specificity or reference, the grain problem, and lack of factualness or normativity. We will then briefly summarize the state of empirical research which has looked at the statistical relationship between DRF and behavior. We suggest that these many flaws mean that they cannot play meaningful explanatory or treatment planning roles, at least not in their current state.

Keywords Dynamic risk factor conceptualization · Measurement of risk

The conceptualization of dynamic risk factors (DRF) and the explanation of offending through the development of theory are pressing concerns for the field of forensic psychology. While statistical relationships are necessary in the prediction of outcomes, without theoretical elaboration they are unable to increase our understanding of crime. It has been suggested that "while a great deal is known about risk factors for offending, less is known about causes, or about causal pathways or mechanisms. Ideally, interventions should target causes of offending" (Farrington, Loeber, & Ttofi, 2012, p. 62). The simple reason for this is that "manipulating a predictor will not change the outcome, while manipulating a cause could" (Wikström & Treiber, 2017, p. 74). One of the virtues of good theories is that they enable us to intervene and influence the causes of behavior. As discussed in the previous chapter, in practice DRF are routinely treated as if they are causes of crime, highlighting a lack of attention to the difference between prediction and explanation. Appreciating the fact that correlation does not necessarily indicate causation, we suggest that the

R. Heffernan, T. Ward, *Dynamic Risk Factors for Sexual Offending: Causal Considerations*, SpringerBriefs in Psychology,
https://doi.org/10.1007/978-3-030-58275-3_2

reliance on predictors in treatment and as the focus of theories is misguided. Perhaps a more useful way forward is to develop explanations of offending which account for the frequent co-existence of DRF but do not solely rely on them as explanations for behavior. Before we discuss this possibility, it is necessary to further explore the extent of the problems with DRF. As discussed in the previous chapter, DRF play a central role in contemporary explanations of crime and rehabilitation; they were identified for prediction purposes and then imported into the generation and development of theory. This chapter will explore the conceptual problems with DRF which make them poor candidates for causal explanation. In our view, they are poor explanatory concepts, and strictly speaking, fail to reliably identify casual processes in both individuals and the social world. We will outline a number of conceptual criticisms of DRF and offer some comments about their potential role in explanations of offending, setting the scene for the following chapter, which outlines a potential way forward by reformulating DRF.

2.1 Conceptual/Theoretical Problems

There are numerous conceptual problems which undermine the putative causal status of DRF. The first is that they *lack coherence* because they are *composite constructs* containing several different types of variable (Ward & Fortune, 2016). While it is likely that they contain causal elements, they are more like general categories or clusters that contain contextual (e.g., gang membership), behavioral (e.g., substance abuse), and psychological state (e.g., attitudes, emotions) aspects. Secondly, because of the frequent co-existence of different DRF and their various potential causal strands, they *lack specificity*. This means it is unclear which potential causes are relevant for explaining the co-existence of any number of DRF and offending. It is also possible that specific features within a DRF category are incompatible or conflicting. For example, lack of intimacy with adults is applied to both those who desire intimacy with other adults but cannot meet this need (e.g., blockage due to interpersonal problems) and those who do not desire intimacy with adults (e.g., due to a preference for children), these represent quite different problems (Mann, Hanson, & Thornton, 2010).

Thirdly, DRF suffer from the *grain problem* or a lack of consensus concerning the appropriate level of abstraction to interpret them at. This is reflected in their formulation at various levels dependent on the context and purpose. For example, as general or "umbrella" domains (e.g., antisocial personality or intimacy deficits) or more fine-grained categories containing specific features (e.g., impulsivity, hostility, entitlement). Finally, DRF *lack factualness* because they are dependent on norms and value judgments rather than being objective or 'scientific kinds' (Ward, 2016). They are (at least partially) normative constructs, which came about due to their correlation with behaviors which are deemed harmful and/or unlawful.

In order to make the four problems listed above more concrete, we will apply them to an example DRF category. The presence of 'intimacy deficits' has a strong empirical association with sexual recidivism and is based on contextual features such as not having a stable intimate relationship presently or in the past or having relationships with high levels of conflict and/or infidelity (Mann et al., 2010; Thornton, 2013). This broad category applies to both individuals who desire and those who avoid intimacy, and it is acknowledged that "these varying facets of dysfunctional intimacy may have different underlying pathologies and so may lead to different treatment targets" (Mann et al., 2010, p. 201). It is also worth noting that the absence of intimacy may relate to the presence of other DRF, such as sexual preoccupation or deviance, insecure attachment, and problems with emotion-regulation (Mann et al., 2010). Therefore, it is uncertain what exactly intimacy deficits are and how they may increase the likelihood that an individual would commit a sexual offence (i.e., the category *lacks specificity*). Further, appropriate intimacy is *normative*, as ideal levels of intimacy may vary across the population (and between populations); intimacy levels are only considered risk factors when observed to co-exist with serious norm violations such as sexual offending. As risk factors like intimacy deficits are normatively defined, they are contextually bound and may function in different ways for different people and in different cultures (Schmidt, Heffernan, & Ward, 2020). In other words, a particular capacity or trait could be considered risky or protective depending on the way that it is used. For example, an individual's ability to make friends easily could be used for prosocial or antisocial means (e.g., building prosocial relationships or grooming a child). The same applies to self-regulation abilities, some people who commit offences are impulsive whereas others are meticulous in planning their offending (i.e., self-regulation is successful, it is just used to engage in harmful or antisocial actions). This is because DRF are simply domains of functioning, they are not inherently a problem, they become "risky" when they are associated with offending.

To illustrate the other two problems listed above, *lack of coherence* and *the grain problem*, we will demonstrate the composite nature of intimacy deficits. The features which hang together across levels of analysis (i.e., from general categories to specific processes) to cause or constitute this DRF may include (but are not limited to):

- *Cultural level*: relationship and gender norms, laws (e.g., age of consent), social opportunities.
- *Interpersonal level*: social skills, learning and reinforcement, social support, social roles and responsibilities.
- *Psychological level*: emotion, beliefs/thoughts about relationships and self (e.g., as unlovable, entitled), attitudes towards others, attachment style.
- *Neurological level*: neurotransmitters (e.g., oxytocin, vasopressin), pre-frontal cortex, hormones.
- *Biological level*: biological sex, arousal, health, physical functioning and attributes (i.e., size, attractiveness).

Each of these levels of analysis would draw from different types of evidence (e.g., behavioral observation at the societal or individual level, self-report, measuring brain/physical processes) and they each represent an important and valid perspective on the problem of 'intimacy deficits'. This general category of deficit or problem contains more detailed features at lower levels, such as emotional, cognitive, and physiological processes. Unique properties emerge across the various levels; no level can alone offer a complete explanation for variation in levels of intimacy and what constitutes a deficit. The examples listed above illustrate the range of processes underpinning one DRF category, and they also highlight the significant overlap among DRF categories (e.g., cognitive, interpersonal, emotional, and sexual). In addition, the mix of different kinds of construct within each DRF category causes incoherence. This incoherence suggests that DRF categories are not suitable to guide explanations of offending. They may be acceptable predictors, but if they are to be transported into the domains of treatment (via case formulation) and explanation (via theory) then they must be further analyzed. While we think that DRF domains contain possible causal processes, due to overly general descriptions it is not currently possible to identify any specific cause. For example, it is not clear whether intimacy deficits might be caused by sexual deviance (i.e., attraction to children), over-sensitivity to interpersonal threat, hostility towards women, emotional congruence with children, a lack of social skills, and so on.

To summarize, DRF are broad, composite categories that lack specificity, contain multiple (sometimes conflicting) concepts, and are overly general (Fortune & Ward, 2017). Each construct is comprised of a range of internal and external characteristics, including underlying propensities and observable manifestations of these within various contexts. The second fundamental issue is that the features and processes that DRF refer to are defined by their statistical relationship to a range of outcomes (i.e., different types of reoffending) within large groups. This means that not only are they normative in the sense that they are defined in terms of their relationship to harmful and illegal behaviors (i.e., they are not scientific, natural, or 'real' categories), but also that they point to trends across populations rather than causes of individual behavior. In this sense they are predictive rather than explanatory tools. They do not refer to genuine causes of crime and thus cannot point to theoretically or personally meaningful targets for correctional treatment. We have also touched upon the dual nature of DRF and PF as contextually bound; they are risky or protective based on their influence upon individuals within certain contexts rather than being fixed causes (Fortune & Ward, 2017). These observations cast significant doubt upon the idea that DRF can interact in order to influence individual behavior and undermine our assumptions about the nature of risk. This further suggests that we are mistaken in our near exclusive focus on correlates of criminal behavior and our tendency to view these as the causes of crime.

2.2 The Measurement of DRF and Change

Numerous studies have focused on the measurement of DRF, their ability to predict offending related outcomes, and detecting changes over time. There are a number of measurement issues which are often cited in these studies, including relying on recidivism as an outcome variable, a lack of attention to inter-rater reliability, an inability to control for extraneous variables, variation in methods for measuring change, and questions about construct validity (Beech, Wakeling, Szumski, & Freemantle, 2016; Beggs, 2010; Cording, Beggs Christofferson, & Grace, 2016). We will not expand upon these issues here, it is enough to note that the methods of measuring DRF and change are imperfect, and there is not yet a consensus on the best way to conduct these evaluations. However, this type of research is currently the closest thing we have to an understanding of the statistical relationships between these variables, it is flawed but gives us some indication. We will now briefly summarize the findings of a recent review (Heffernan, Wegerhoff, & Ward, 2019) which asked three questions, what is the evidence that: (1) DRF change over time, (2) changes predict variation in recidivism outcomes, and (3) treatment targeting DRF mediates this relationship? It is clear that if there is a causal relationship between DRF and reoffending, we should observe that when DRF change, so do rates of offending. This observation would give us some confidence that we should focus on DRF in order to develop causal explanations of offending. Further, it would support the premise of the need principle, that DRF are the appropriate targets for interventions to reduce crime. We now turn our attention to each of these three questions.

Firstly, it is important that researchers determine whether DRF can and do change over time, otherwise they are not truly dynamic and there is little point targeting them in correctional programs. It is clear that many DRF are theoretically able to shift, people can change who they associate with, they can engage in more prosocial leisure pursuits and gain employment, and attitudes can shift over time. There are numerous studies which have shown that shifts in these factors can be detected, often following intervention (e.g., Beggs, 2010; Kingston & Olver, 2018; O'Brien & Daffern, 2017; Olver, Nicholaichuk, & Wong, 2014; Olver & Wong, 2011). However, others have found that certain factors seem to change more than others (Brooks Holliday, Heilbrun, & Fretz, 2012; Greiner, Law, & Brown, 2015; Labrecque, Smith, Lovins, & Latessa, 2014; Schlager & Pacheco, 2011; Wooditch, Tang, & Taxman, 2014), however, the presumed source of change (i.e., as a result of or independent of treatment) seems to vary across studies. These findings suggest that changes in DRF over time do occur to some degree and that these changes can be measured. However, we cannot rule out the possibility of measurement error influencing changes to scores in any particular study. This possibility is often suggested when static factors show change (e.g., Labrecque et al., 2014; Schlager & Pacheco, 2011), but the same is not considered for DRF due to the assumption that they can and will change. Unfortunately, even if we can confirm that DRF change, due to their composite nature we cannot be sure what exactly is influencing this observed change.

Secondly, Andrews and Bonta's (2010) suggestion that criminogenic needs are those factors which when altered result in changes to behavior (e.g., reduced recidivism) is central to the need principle of the RNR model. If changes in DRF are not associated with reductions in recidivism, then there would be little point targeting them in treatment. To consider one meta-analysis which has investigated this issue, Serin, Lloyd, Helmus, Derkzen, and Luong (2013) found support for the relationship between changes in DRF scores and reductions in recidivism. However, only

27 per cent of the possible effect sizes were significant and many of the DRF did not demonstrate the expected relationships, Serin et al. conclude that "little is confidently known about which factors are the most productive targets for change, whether DRF truly behave in a dynamic way to affect future recidivism, and if change predicts recidivism beyond knowledge of static risk" (p. 50). While the links that they did find were promising, these results suggest that the relationship between specific DRF and recidivism may not be as straight forward nor strong as is often assumed. Numerous individual studies which have looked at this same issue have found mixed results, for example, a study by Olver, Nicholaichuk, Kingston, and Wong (2014) found "very small to moderate" changes to DRF and concluded that these were "weakly and inconsistently" related to reoffending (p. 544). Overall, it seems that the evidence to support the relationship between DRF change and reduced recidivism is questionable.

Third, we consider the question of whether treatment mediates this change. Is it the case that programmes targeting DRF result in lower DRF ratings (i.e., proximal measures) and reductions in reoffending? One might hope so, however, the evidence for this is also mixed. To illustrate we will briefly consider three reviews. Beggs (2010) reviewed studies measuring within treatment changes and found mixed results, concluding that, despite some promising findings, there is limited and inconsistent evidence that within-treatment changes to DRF are associated with reductions in reoffending (particularly when measured psychometrically). Olver and Wong's (2013) review also found mixed results. Overall, more change during treatment seemed to be associated with larger reductions in reoffending, however, Olver and Wong concluded that changes made in treatment may or may not be directly related to risk. Finally, Serin et al. (2013) observed an inconsistent relationship between treatment change and recidivism and concluded that it is "difficult to defend successful programs when it is unclear which treatment elements are responsible for the change and which offenders have changed" (p. 50). This supports our earlier claim, that even if treatment seems to support our goal of reducing crime, it is important for future development of interventions that we are able to isolate and determine which aspects of treatment are influencing this outcome and how this occurs. Otherwise it is difficult to generalize results to other contexts and ensure that the most effective parts of interventions are being prioritized. Further, if we assume that DRF change is the mechanism through which treatment influences future behavior, then we must develop a better understanding of what these are and how and why they change over time. If we fail to do this our progress in reducing recidivism and preventing harm will stall and we will be unable to improve upon the success of existing rehabilitation programs.

Finally, researchers have recently become interested in the interrelationships of DRF and pathways to crime. For example, van den Berg et al. (2020) conducted a network analysis on the relationship between DRF (in individuals convicted of sexual offences) and offending, and found that these relationships varied across the different DRF. Specifically, they "identified clusters involving sexual self-regulation, emotionally intimate relationships, antisocial traits, and self-management skills" (p. 12). Further, they found that several DRF occupied central positions within networks: general rejection/loneliness, poor cognitive problem-solving, and impulsive acts (this factor displayed the strongest independent relationship with reoffending). They suggest that these three factors could be considered bridging factors between DRF clusters and suggest that their findings have theoretical implications (i.e., to the extent that they indicate causal interactions). Research such as this is a step in the right direction and has the potential to aid researchers in testing hypotheses about the relationship between certain phenomena and offending. It may also help to uncover which DRF have the greatest influence on behavior and thus which should be emphasized in treatment. However, we suggest that the phenomena of interest (i.e., DRF) are currently too vague and broad to provide useful information about the causal processes underpinning these inter-relationships and linking them with behavior.

2.3 Summary

This chapter has explored a number of conceptual and empirical problems with DRF. Conceptual issues largely stem from the composite nature of DRF, the fact that they are comprised of a mixture of psychological features, states, and contexts, rather than being one coherent concept. We used the example of 'intimacy deficits' to illustrate this issue and other related problems, such as the lack of reference to causal processes and the grain problem. In addition, we highlighted that DRF are in part normative constructs; they are defined in relation to undesirable or crime-related outcomes and they may or may not be risk factors depending on the presence of other features (of the person and their environment). We then briefly summarized recent empirical literature which has investigated the relationship between DRF change and reoffending. Based on the conclusions of reviews and meta-analyses in this field, we suggest that the evidence for a clear link between treatment, DRF change, and behavioral change is currently mixed and inconclusive. The conceptual and empirical problems discussed in this chapter paint a picture of an indirect relationship between DRF and offending. For this reason, we believe DRF cannot possibly be considered causal or explanatory constructs. However, given their strong association with crime, they arguably have a role to play in the explanation of offending.

References

Andrews, D. A., & Bonta, J. (2010). *The psychology of criminal conduct* (5th ed.). New Providence, NJ: LexisNexis.

Beech, A. R., Wakeling, H. C., Szumski, F., & Freemantle, N. (2016). Problems in the measurement of dynamic risk factors in sexual offenders. *Psychology, Crime & Law, 22*(1–2), 68–83. https://doi.org/10.1080/1068316x.2015.1109095

Beggs, S. (2010). Within-treatment outcome among sexual offenders: A review. *Aggression and Violent Behavior, 15*(5), 369–379. https://doi.org/10.1016/j.avb.2010.06.005

Brooks Holliday, S., Heilbrun, K., & Fretz, R. (2012). Examining improvements in criminogenic needs: The risk reduction potential of a structured re-entry program. *Behavioral Sciences & the Law, 30*(4), 431–447. https://doi.org/10.1002/bsl.2016

Cording, J. R., Beggs Christofferson, S. M., & Grace, R. C. (2016). Challenges for the theory and application of dynamic risk factors. *Psychology, Crime & Law, 22*(1–2), 84–103. https://doi.org/10.1080/1068316x.2015.1111367

Farrington, D. P., Loeber, R., & Ttofi, M. M. (2012). Risk and protective factors for offending. In B. C. Welsh & D. P. Farrington (Eds.), *The Oxford handbook of crime prevention* (pp. 46–69). New York, NY: Oxford university Press.

Fortune, C.-A., & Ward, T. (2017). Problems in protective factor research and practice. *Aggression and Violent Behavior, 32*, 1–3. https://doi.org/10.1016/j.avb.2016.12.008

Greiner, L. E., Law, M. A., & Brown, S. L. (2015). Using dynamic factors to predict recidivism among women: A four-wave prospective study. *Criminal Justice and Behavior, 42*(5), 457–480. https://doi.org/10.1177/0093854814553222

Kingston, D. A., & Olver, M. E. (2018). Psychometric examination of treatment change among mentally disordered offenders: A risk–needs analysis. *Criminal Justice and Behavior, 45*(2), 153–172. https://doi.org/10.1177/0093854817743539

Labrecque, R. M., Smith, P., Lovins, B. K., & Latessa, E. J. (2014). The importance of reassessment: How changes in the LSI-R risk score can improve the prediction of recidivism. *Journal of Offender Rehabilitation, 53*(2), 116–128. https://doi.org/10.1080/10509674.2013.868389

Mann, R. E., Hanson, R. K., & Thornton, D. (2010). Assessing risk for sexual recidivism: Some proposals on the nature of psychologically meaningful risk factors. *Sexual Abuse, 22*(2), 191–217. https://doi.org/10.1177/1079063210366039

O'Brien, K., & Daffern, M. (2017). Treatment gain in violent offenders: The relationship between proximal outcomes, risk reduction and violent recidivism. *Psychiatry, Psychology and Law, 24*(2), 244–258. https://doi.org/10.1080/13218719.2016.1209804

Olver, M. E., Nicholaichuk, T. P., Kingston, D. A., & Wong, S. C. P. (2014). A multisite examination of sexual violence risk and therapeutic change. *Journal of Consulting and Clinical Psychology, 82*(2), 312–324. https://doi.org/10.1037/a0035340

Olver, M. E., Nicholaichuk, T. P., & Wong, S. C. (2014). The predictive and convergent validity of a psychometric battery used to assess sexual offenders in a treatment programme: An 18-year follow-up. *Journal of Sexual Aggression, 20*(2), 216–239. https://doi.org/10.1080/13552600.2013.816791

Olver, M. E., & Wong, S. C. P. (2011). A comparison of static and dynamic assessment of sexual offender risk and need in a treatment context. *Criminal Justice and Behavior, 38*(2), 113–126. https://doi.org/10.1177/0093854810389534

Olver, M. E., & Wong, S. C. P. (2013). Treatment programs for high risk sexual offenders: Program and offender characteristics, attrition, treatment change and recidivism. *Aggression and Violent Behavior, 18*(5), 579–591. https://doi.org/10.1016/j.avb.2013.06.002

Schlager, M. D., & Pacheco, D. (2011). An examination of changes in LSI-R scores over time: Making the case for needs-based case management. *Criminal Justice and Behavior, 38*(6), 541–553. https://doi.org/10.1177/0093854811402300

Schmidt, S., Heffernan, R., & Ward, T. (2020). Why we cannot explain cross-cultural differences in risk assessment. *Aggression and Violent Behavior, 50*, 1–12. https://doi.org/10.1016/j.avb.2019.101346

Serin, R. C., Lloyd, C. D., Helmus, L., Derkzen, D. M., & Luong, D. (2013). Does intra-individual change predict offender recidivism? Searching for the holy grail in assessing offender change. *Aggression and Violent Behavior, 18*(1), 32–53. https://doi.org/10.1016/j.avb.2012.09.002

Thornton, D. (2013). Implications of our developing understanding of risk and protective factors in the treatment of adult male sexual offenders. *International Journal of Behavioral Consultation and Therapy, 8*, 62–65.

van den Berg, J. W., Smid, W., Kossakowski, J. J., van Beek, D., Borsboom, D., Janssen, E., & Gijs, L. (2020). The application of network analysis to dynamic risk factors in adult male sex offenders. *Clinical Psychological Science*. https://doi.org/10.1177/2167702620901720

Ward, T. (2016). Dynamic risk factors: Scientific kinds or predictive constructs. *Psychology, Crime & Law, 22*(1–2), 2–16. https://doi.org/10.1080/1068316x.2015.1109094

Ward, T., & Fortune, C.-A. (2016). The role of dynamic risk factors in the explanation of offending. *Aggression and Violent Behavior, 29*, 79–88. https://doi.org/10.1016/j.avb.2016.06.007

Wikström, P. O. H., & Treiber, K. (2017). Beyond risk factors: An analytical approach to crime prevention. In B. Teasdale & M. S. Bradley (Eds.), *Preventing crime and violence* (pp. 73–87). Cham, Switzerland: Springer.

Wooditch, A., Tang, L. L., & Taxman, F. S. (2014). Which criminogenic need changes are most important in promoting desistance from crime and substance use? *Criminal Justice and Behavior, 41*(3), 276–299. https://doi.org/10.1177/0093854813503543

Chapter 3
Reformulating Dynamic Risk Factors

Abstract We have so far argued that the relationship between dynamic risk factors (DRF) and offending is not as straight-forward as commonly presumed, and therefore they cannot be considered causes of behavior. In this chapter we draw from current research in the domains of psychopathology classification and treatment, and medical epidemiology to formulate a set of methodological guidelines to help researchers translate DRF into explanatory constructs. The aim of this chapter is to outline the ways in which these offence correlates can be utilised within explanations of behavior. There is clearly an association between these factors and offending, but as argued in the previous chapter it should not be assumed that this is a causal relationship.

Keywords Dynamic risk factor reconceptualization, explaining offending · Boundary objects

As explored in the previous chapter, there are empirical and conceptual considerations when inferring a causal relationship between DRF and outcomes such as recidivism. We suggested that the relationship between DRF and offending cannot be considered causal, because of the presence of significant conceptual and empirical problems. This chapter will explore what the nature of this relationship may be and what role DRF might play within future explanations of offending. We begin by discussing the targets of explanation and the nature and functions of classification in forensic psychology. We continue by exploring a set of causal criteria put forward by Bradford-Hill (1965) and, drawing from the conclusions of the previous chapter, summarize the ability of DRF to satisfy these. We then, building on the recent focus on agency in theories of offending, introduce an approach to DRF which is based on the concept of 'boundary objects' and suggest that this perspective has merit in recognizing the normative nature of DRF and explaining their relationship with

R. Heffernan, T. Ward, *Dynamic Risk Factors for Sexual Offending: Causal Considerations*, SpringerBriefs in Psychology,
https://doi.org/10.1007/978-3-030-58275-3_3

behavior. We conclude this chapter by outlining some recent suggestions for theory development which are utilised throughout the remainder of this book.

3.1 Classification

It is important that any theoretical research project begins with a clear description of what is to be explained, that is, the targets of explanation. In the criminal justice context, it makes sense that the focus of explanation should be the behavior that we wish to change, although it is acknowledged that 'crime' is a broad and value-laden category containing various actions and outcomes (Ward, 2019). Since there are a set of correlates that are commonly relied upon to predict future offending, any comprehensive explanation of crime should also be able to explain the frequent but varied co-occurrence of DRF. There are numerous examples of these behaviors and characteristics (i.e., DRF) contained within etiological theories, lists of correlates such as the central eight (Andrews & Bonta, 2010), assessment tools, treatment manuals, and literature from related areas such as criminology and developmental psychology. The reason DRF are included as explanatory targets alongside offending behavior is that some of them (e.g., attitudes, propensities, abilities) are currently the closest thing we have to psychologically meaningful features of offending (Mann, Hanson, & Thornton, 2010). However, we emphasize the importance of explaining offending behavior over its correlates, as DRF do not always accompany offending in typical ways, and indeed many of these characteristics may be present in the general population—they are human attributes independent of crime.

In other, more advanced branches of science, classification relies on the identification of 'natural kinds' (Magnus, 2012). Natural kinds can be defined as categories which facilitate "inductive and explanatory success" (Magnus, 2012, p. 48); further properties may be inferred following the classification of entities within these 'natural' categories. Thus, this kind of classification picks out real things which exist independent of human understanding. For example, in classifying an animal as a species one can infer typical life span, behaviors, diet, physical attributes, and so on. The classification system of 'species' picks out natural kinds and thus allows one to make predictions and causal attributions for particular behaviors. For this reason, natural kinds are useful targets for generating explanatory theories.

However, this type of inference is not possible in the field of forensic psychology, where individuals are often classified or grouped according to their offence type or the presence of DRF (Ward, Durrant, & Dixon, in press, a; see the special issue on the classification of crime edited by Ward, Durrant, & Dixon, in press, b). For example, if you know that Tom is a 'sexual offender', you cannot reliably infer anything other than that he is a person who has engaged in an illegal behavior of a sexual nature which has resulted in a conviction. Even though it may be more likely that he has deviant sexual interests compared to the general population, this is not necessarily the case—there is no DRF with a strong enough relationship with recidivism that its presence could be inferred simply through an individual's classification by offence type. Types of offending (e.g., violent, dishonesty, sexual) are based on general categories of behavior and do not account for diverse motivations and causal processes. They represent legal categories which reflect moral judgments about the harm caused by certain kinds of action. Thus, they are normative rather than natural or scientific kinds, which means that they are not valid targets for explanation (Ward & Carter, 2019). Classification of individuals via the presence of DRF suffers from the same problems due to their normative nature. They are hybrid or composite categories typically composed of clusters of varying problems that do not 'hang together' in any meaningful sense.

For this reason, theories based on DRF and types of offending arguably lack the ability to pick out mechanisms and processes which could plausibly cause behavior. Offence categories and DRF do not exist in any real sense, they are value-laden concepts based on social norms (Ward & Heffernan, 2017). This is reflected in the diversity of motivations and behaviors within offence categories and the substantial overlap between offence categories and other related problems—for example, drug and alcohol use, relationship instability. The categories of 'sex offender' and 'violent offender' are so general that we are unable to make useful inferences about the causes of these actions based on these classifications. This represents a significant problem for theorists in this field, the classification systems available are not fit for purpose, they were identified via normative judgments and do not pick out scientific or natural kinds (Ward & Carter, 2019). Persons who commit crimes or experience the kinds of problems represented by DRF do not possess a unique set of characteristics or causal processes underpinning their behavior. They are not fundamentally different from other human beings and so the causes of their behavior are unlikely to be unique or specific to offending. Rather, the reasons why an 'offender' commits a crime may be the same as the reasons for any other goal-directed behavior by any other person. One may wonder why we would bother constructing an explanation directed at any specific offence (or any other category of behavior).

Furthermore, there are strong grounds for believing that it is not possible to arrive at a *one size fits all* way of classifying things within any scientific domain. Rather, taking into account the different levels of analysis for empirical phenomena, and the varying tasks that researchers and practitioners are faced with, classificatory pluralism seems like the most promising way to proceed (Carter, Ward, & Strauss-Hughes, in press). Trying to come up with a single, overarching classification system that can satisfy all of the different epistemic tasks facing researchers within this field (i.e., prediction, intervention, explanation) is arguably a poor strategy. Thus, there are likely to be varying systems for constructing and grouping categories together depending on the epistemic task; a system that is suitable for risk prediction may not be optimal for guiding treatment (Carter et al., in press).

From a treatment perspective, Ward and Carter (2019) recently suggested that explanations would be better directed towards the motivational or functional systems which underpin certain types of practice (e.g., emotion management, threat detection, mate seeking), rather than the outcomes or behaviors themselves (e.g., violence, sexual abuse). This is because the same action may have a range of reasons or causes, and different behaviors may be caused by the same underlying mechanisms. For example, problems with social interactions may be partially caused by an overly active threat detection mechanism, which may manifest in terms of social isolation, social phobia, violence, sexual offending, substance abuse, and so on. Thus, these behaviors do not warrant separate explanations. The way problems manifest will depend on the functioning of the underlying causal mechanisms, as well as environmental opportunities and constraints. One way to overcome this issue is to shift the focus of explanation to behaviors more generally, and then to apply these explanations to various criminal behaviors and their co-existing problems (i.e., explaining why features such as intimacy problems and sexual deviance *often* accompany sexual offending). In other words, while in the criminal justice domain we are concerned with preventing particular types of norm violation (i.e., offence types and associated DRF), it is important that explanations draw upon the mechanisms underpinning human functioning in general. These explanations are more likely to tap into natural kinds or real features of persons and behavior (as opposed to 'offenders' and offences).

It is important to set out the focus of enquiry in a clear and considered way, appreciating that our explanatory pursuits are influenced by social and ethical values. For example, the value of developing explanations of the sexual abuse of children is that it may inform practice, either to prevent sexual abuse from happening in the first place or to stop it from reoccurring after an individual has already committed an offence. If we understand why it happens, we can predict and ideally reduce the likelihood of future offending. Next, we need to describe what it is we hope to explain. Clearly, we cannot hope to develop one explanation for sexual offending and every possible behavior and causal process which may be contained within this category—the category is simply too broad. Instead we need to develop more fine-grained *exemplars* which represent typical sets of problems which tend to co-occur. In the context of mental illness, Murphy (2016) defines an *exemplar* as follows:

> An exemplar is a representation of the typical course and symptoms of a mental illness, whereas a model is a representation of those symptoms, that course, and the causal determinants of both of them. A model is an exemplar together with an explanation. (p. 206)

For example, an exemplar might describe a person who has a sexual preference for prepubescent children, who has fantasized about and engaged in sex with children, who reports that they emotionally identify with children, and believes that children are capable of consenting to and enjoying sex (Mann et al., 2010; Ward, 2014). This exemplar does not apply to every person who has committed a sexual offence against children, instead it represents a sub-category of persons who have engaged in this behavior and experience problems with sexual and emotional attraction to children. If the goal is prevention of sexual abuse, multiple exemplars must be developed, each representing a pattern of sexual offending. For example, capturing varying offence pathways, problem clusters, symptoms, and motivations (i.e., typologies). These should better capture the complexity of individual presentations, while also reflecting common processes.

3.2 Causal Criteria

We have suggested that the central role of DRF within explanations of offending depends on the extent to which they can be considered causally related to sexual offending. In order to explore this more systematically, we will now consider a set of causal criteria from the epidemiological literature. Bradford-Hill (1965) put forward nine criteria which can assist researchers in determining causal relationships, which are:

1. Strong *statistical association* with a specific outcome
2. *Consistency* (i.e.., across places, circumstances, time, and observers)
3. *Specificity* (i.e., to particular groups, body systems and sites, and diseases)
4. *Temporality* (i.e., a putative cause precedes an outcome)
5. *Biological gradient* (i.e., a decrease in effect with a decrease in cause)
6. *Plausibility* (i.e., is the cause reasonable within the context of current knowledge? Ideally an etiological/causal mechanism should be identified)
7. *Coherence* (i.e., does it cohere with knowledge about the domain? Established facts act as epistemic constraints on causal inference)
8. *Experimental* manipulation (i.e., evidence from well-designed studies supports a cause and effect relationship)
9. *Analogy* (i.e., the existence of other similar causal relationships)

The extent to which DRF meet these criteria has been somewhat explored in the previous chapter (also see, Ward & Fortune, 2016). To summarize, the ability of DRF to predict recidivism at a level better than chance suggests that there is a statistical *association* between these constructs and recidivism. This is likely to be stronger for some DRF than others. Their *consistency* across contexts and raters has also been demonstrated to some degree, however, their cross-cultural utility has been seriously questioned (Schmidt, Heffernan, & Ward, 2020; Shepherd & Lewis-Fernandez, 2016), and inter-rater reliability varies by factor, for example, "items requiring greater subjective judgment, such as marital/family factors, use of leisure time, and peer relationships, have significantly lower reported rates of reliability" (Baird, 2009, p. 7). Thus, criteria one and two have been partially met, but we would argue not adequately.

The *specificity* of DRF to both individuals who have committed offences and offending contexts is also unsupported. For example, relationship issues, alcohol abuse, and poor self-regulation or impulsivity are experienced by individuals in the general (i.e., largely non-offending) population, indeed even specific factors like pedophilia may be observed in individuals who have not engaged in sexually abusive behavior. However, some offence-related attitudes and emotions and use of illegal substances may be more specific to offending. This is partially due to their normative nature and the fact that they are defined in relation to the criterion (i.e., they are offence-supportive or offences themselves). In light of these normative issues, we suggest that criteria three has not been met.

In regard to criteria four, longitudinal studies have demonstrated that DRF *temporally* precede recidivism. However, the extent to which they were present prior to the initial offence has not been established for all DRF. Therefore, perhaps some DRF function as maintaining factors of criminal lifestyles rather than initial causes of offending. For example, an individual may develop errors in thinking or gravitate towards antisocial peers following incarceration, but perhaps they were not present during the initial offence. Arguably, if the outcome is recidivism rather than the initial onset of offending, then DRF meet criteria four. The *biological gradient* (i.e., increases and decreases in recidivism) and *experimental manipulation* (i.e., through treatment) of DRF were briefly explored in chapter two, and the relationship was not found to be linear; therefore, we suggest that criteria five and eight are not adequately supported.

In terms of the *plausibility* of DRF as causes of offending, the description of functional relationships between DRF and offending (i.e., the PCC) gives a superficial account of their relationship. However, as discussed in the previous chapter, it falls short of specifying etiological or causal mechanisms. In addition, some DRF are easier to link with crime than others, for instance antisocial attitudes and personality are more plausible causes of crime than unemployment and relationship issues (i.e., the latter may be symptomatic of these problems, or be more normative and related to behaviors other than crime). Therefore, criteria six has not been fully met, DRF require further specification in order to be considered plausible causes. For example, in order for relationship issues or interpersonal problems to be a plausible cause of violent behavior we would need to identify what the problem is (e.g., communication, expectations, jealousy or fear of abandonment) and how it is linked with violence (i.e., the function of violence such as control or emotion expression, whether this process was planned or impulsive). This level of specificity requires theories which refer to psychological mechanisms and processes.

Further, as discussed above, DRF are themselves composite constructs, which undermines their ability to be considered *coherent* with existing knowledge about offending. However, they may be considered coherent with the broader knowledge about the domain (i.e., the PCC and other theories of crime), the reason for this being that they are often the basis of these theories. Therefore, criterion seven, coherence, may be partially met, but this may be a side effect of the reliance on these correlates as explanations for crime. Finally, the criterion of *analogy* (criterion nine) or the existence of similar causal relationships has not been met. For instance, there is a lack of mechanistic or causal explanations linking psychological phenomena and behaviors in related disciplines such as psychopathology (i.e., the debate surrounding psychological symptoms and disorders).

In conclusion, while DRF may temporally precede and be statistically associated with recidivism (to a degree), they fail to demonstrate the expected relationships and fall short of being plausible causes and coherent explanations for crime. One of the reasons for this is their value-laden nature; definitions of DRF and crime rely on social norms and expectations. Part of the process of theory generation (and development) is the determination of suitable targets for these explanations, and as discussed earlier, the current targets (DRF) are value-laden concepts. We suggest that in order to progress our understanding of the causes of offending we need to shift our focus away from DRF and towards behavior more generally, only then can we understand how DRF and offending are related.

3.3 Agency Approaches

We will now offer an approach to theory development which views DRF and offending as aspects of personal agency and goal-directed action. This shift may help to address the normative nature of DRF and offending, as it is focused on what people do and why they do it—it can account for norms and value judgments because they are embedded within the behavioral practices which make up human life. This is not dissimilar to Ward and Carter's (2019) suggestion that explanations be directed at particular motivational systems. Agency is the ability to initiate, and process of engaging in, intentional goal-directed behavior. The kinds of practices humans engage in reflect their needs and priorities, and they are enabled by a set of capacities. For example, a set of practices aimed at attaining sexual intimacy may include seeking a companion for a date, impressing them with conversational skills or physical attractiveness or vocational success, seeking consent, and so on. For individuals who have deficits (either temporary or enduring) in any of the capacities necessary to engage in these practices (e.g., self-regulation, communication skills, intelligence), other options will be sought. In some cases, this may lead to offending, in other cases it may lead to other problems (e.g., social anxiety, loneliness, substance use). The idea is that offences are practices aimed at particular outcomes and so in order to understand why this has occurred we need to look at the ideal conditions (i.e., successful practices) and what has gone wrong in situations where offending has occurred.

3.4 Suggestions for Theory Development

We will now outline several suggestions for theory development which have informed the methodological framework we sketch out in the following chapter. In addition to clearly outlining the targets of explanation, it is suggested that researchers *deconstruct* DRF and attempt to extract any potential causal mechanisms contained within these broad categories. This would begin to address the composite nature of DRF, their incoherence, and lack of specificity. Further, it is suggested that researchers utilize the method of integrative pluralism, linking theories across various levels of explanation. This would begin to address the grain problem, as it incorporates finer grains of analysis. Finally, in order to link DRF with behavior it is suggested that these are located within a theory of goal-directed behavior or agency. This ensures that normativity is acknowledged and, as DRF are dispersed across patterns of behavior, the links between causal mechanisms, DRF, and behavior become clearer.

Firstly, keeping in mind the normativity of DRF (i.e., their lack of factualness), researchers must make a distinction between the search for factors that *cause* particular outcomes and the *normative* judgments that these outcomes are harmful. This points to the importance of explicitly thinking about different levels of explanation or analysis. For example, those concerning psychological (and biological/neurological) mechanisms versus norms and practices. One way to do this is to adopt a 'levels of analysis' framework such as the *research domain criteria* (RDoC) project from the field of psychopathology classification (Cuthbert & Kozak, 2013; Lilienfeld, 2014; Ward & Fortune, 2016) to guide research into the causal mechanisms generating behavior. Looking to analogue fields such as psychopathology, which is currently facing significant challenges similar to those experienced in forensic psychology (e.g., searching for causal mechanisms, comorbidity, transdiagnostic criteria, etc.), can offer potential avenues for future research.

Adapting the RDoC framework for the field of forensic and correctional psychology, the emphasis would initially be on core psychological domains of functioning such as working memory, self-regulation processes, or negative valance systems and investigating how these may cause crime related problems in certain contexts (Ward & Fortune, 2016). Therefore, the initial locus of explanation would be sub-personal mechanisms underpinning individuals' actions, such as the processes and components comprising working memory or emotion regulation. For example, the discovery that depletion of serotonin levels can result in lowered mood, which in turn might lead to the increased salience of norms associated with sex and intimacy seeking. When investigating these domains of functioning researchers can speak about dysfunction of mechanisms (i.e., instances where they do not function as they should, for example attentional biases, chronic low mood, etc.). These are likely to influence behavior and, in some cases, may be relevant to offending.

The social, ethical, and prudential norms (i.e., personal goals) that direct the practices constituting DRF in everyday life can then be studied separately, in light of the causal information yielded by empirical research into causal mechanisms. Once research attention shifts from sub-personal mechanisms to particular actions constituting DRF such as emotional dysregulation, researchers must consider goal-directed practices, which are constituted by norms and their associated actions. For example, an explanation of child sexual abuse that invokes desire for (and value of) sexual intimacy, rather than lowered serotonin levels. Norm-based explanations are typically formulated in terms of reasons, and reasons track values and beliefs. A reasons-based explanation will refer to agents, actions, and contexts as the preferred units of analysis, rather than underlying psychological or biological mechanisms (Ward et al., in press a). The idea here is that there are multiple valid levels of analysis, all of which have something unique and useful to offer a comprehensive explanation of behavior. Certain levels may be privileged in different practical tasks (e.g., administering medication, treatment, risk management, prevention), but all have a potential role in explanation. The challenge for theoretical researchers then is how to bring all of these perspectives together in a way that is comprehensive but also useful, which contains enough detail but avoids being overly complicated.

Integrative pluralism (Mitchell, 2003) is the methodological process of linking *local theories* across multiple levels of explanation to form comprehensive theoretical structures that can account for a larger range of phenomena. Local theories might focus solely on one psychological mechanism or level of explanation, and thus offer a partial explanation for a phenomenon which can be enriched by being linked with other theories. For example, the way that we explain our own behavior (a subjective first-person perspective) differs from the way that psychological (or biological or sociological) theory would explain our decision-making processes, interpersonal functioning, positive and negative emotional states and traits, and so on (a third person perspective). Each perspective offers a unique explanatory viewpoint which cannot be reduced or eliminated (i.e., important information is lost when social interactions are reduced to neurological processes). For the simple reason that a first-person perspective is the subjective point from which we engage in goal-directed behavior, we propose that this is an important and irreducible level of explanation (Baker, 2015; Ward, 2014, 2016). However, which level is prioritized in any given explanation will depend on the task at hand. For example, in therapy the subjective first-person level of explanation might be most useful, with its focus on experience and meaning, however, when considering the use of medication, neurological and biological levels are more relevant. In addition, social and contextual explanations may assist decision-makers in managing individuals within the community and in environmental strategies to prevent crime.

3.5 DRF as Boundary Objects

Recent theoretical work on classification in correctional and forensic psychology has focused on the kind of objects that DRF are and has gone beyond simply seeing them as summaries of different kinds of factors. Ward et al. (in press b) note that a variety of "objects"[1] are contained within different forensic and correctional classification systems, including disorders (e.g., psychopathy), motives and needs, offending behaviors, cognition, risk factors, offence pathways, and developmental trajectories. More abstractly, the units of analysis can be divided into classification systems that cover the person, their actions across domains and over time, and the contexts within which they offend (for a discussion of boundary objects in forensic psychology see Ward, Durrant, & Dixon, in press b).

A problem arising from the variety of classification systems currently used in the criminal justice field is that it is unclear whether systems built with different units of analysis can be meaningfully compared. This problems extends to within offence

[1] By "object" we include anything that is the unit of classification such as individuals, behaviors, situations, risk factors, and so on.

categories (e.g., types of sex offending) and across different categories of crime (e.g., sexual versus violent offending). For example, typologies of child sexual offending may be centered around types of offence pathways, crime scene characteristics, preferred victims, or sexual arousal patterns. Each type of classification system is focused on a different unit of analysis: sequences of behavior, individual characteristics, or contextual features. To make things more complex, each of these units may be subdivided into more fine-grained ones (individual: sexual preferences, cognitive distortions, levels of behavioral control, personality features, etc.). The question is: are these descriptions of one object (e.g., sexual offending) or multiple, possibly unrelated ones? The conceptual units of each of the classification systems used within correctional systems are different and focus on varying properties and types of objects. This is conceptually confusing and likely to result in increasingly fragmented, uncoordinated research.

One possible solution to the number of classification systems across different types of crime and within offence categories is to utilize the concept of *boundary objects*, developed by the sociologist of science, Leigh Star (Star & Griesemer, 1989). Her work centred on describing the practices of collecting, preparing, and exhibiting animals in the Museum of Vertebrate Zoology, at the University of California, Berkeley. Star was struck by the fact that different professional groups (e.g., scientists, academics, hunters, amateur collectors, patrons, members of the public) saw the objects in the collection in quite distinctive ways and classified them according to their own interests and knowledge bases. This created the puzzle of how best to integrate or at least link their varying viewpoints, and by doing so, further research and practice. Her solution was to invent the concept of a *boundary object* that was both a common representation of an object (a specimen; epistemology) and the object itself (ontology). The reference to the term "boundary" was intended to capture the interdisciplinary, and multiple perspectives of the object; crossing different professional and theoretical boundaries. More specifically:

> Boundary objects are objects which are both plastic enough to adapt to local needs and the constraints of the several parties employing them, yet robust enough to maintain a common identity across sites. They are weakly structured in common use, and become strongly structured in individual site use. These objects may be abstract or concrete. They have different meanings in different social worlds but their structure is common enough to more than one world to make them recognizable, a means of translation. The creation and management of boundary objects is a key process in developing and maintaining coherence across intersecting social worlds (Bowker, Timmermans, Clarke, & Balka, 2015; pp. 176–177).

The common representation of a boundary object is a conceptually thin, abstract one that permits all interested parties to agree that they are dealing with the same object. Each party then develops their own more detailed and concrete representations that flesh out aspects of the boundary object. An example given by Star is that of an general map of a geographical area that all map makers can agree on. Using this common map as an anchor point, different investigators can then design a number of detailed local maps that meet their particular needs, for example, mapping (and classifying) the river systems or natural flora and fauna within that territory (Star & Griesemer, 1989).

The concept of a boundary object can be used to address the conceptual problems associated with DRF. First, different kinds of DRF such as crime supportive attitudes, social skills deficits, emotional regulation problems or deviant sexual interests can be represented using the same basic conceptual unit (i.e., *agent-action-context*) but given a "local" representation in terms of the risk factor it is. Each of the subcomponents comprising this category can be broken down and examined at different grains of analysis, from different theoretical perspectives. For example, the subcomponent of *agent* could be further divided according to types of goals, needs or mental state factors (e.g., desire to have a sexual relationship with children; feeling fearful), or in terms of enduring psychological features (e.g., impaired perspective taking). The subcomponent of *actions* could be classified in terms of processes (e.g., excusing, threatening, interpreting) or offence properties (e.g., grooming, forming pedophilic networks). The *contexts* of DRF would include the norms associated with social roles and situations, and depict why a particular action is viewed as a crime (e.g., sexualized behavior with children, poor self-regulation).

Second, as argued above, the composite nature of DRF has been the focus of critical analysis over the last few years, and they are poor classificatory and explanatory constructs (Carter et al., in press). However, if they are viewed as boundary objects characterized by the agent-action-context schema, they can become a focal point or "hub" for classificatory systems. For example, the DRF of emotional congruence with children has an agent component (e.g., fears of adult rejection, preference for children), an action component (e.g., child oriented activities), and a contextual component (e.g., social norms stipulating how adults should act towards children; access to children), which can all be further subjects of classification.

Third, conceptualizing DRF as boundary objects helps forensic practitioners to shift their attention from just crime to other situations in which crime related problems appear (see Ward & Carter, 2019). For example, the motivational system of fear and security could result directly in violence but also be associated with addiction and mood problems. Classification efforts guided by the idea of boundary objects enables practitioners to converge on the needs and goals of individuals and their relationship to subsequent actions and problem contexts rather than simply focusing on crime. The adoption of the boundary object idea and its ability to function as an abstract object in classification and explanatory practices, allows for different classification systems for different tasks without giving up the idea that they are classifications of the same object.

Fourth, another strength of this approach is the coherence of the concept of a boundary object with current work on scientific classification. Carter et al. (in press) state that "there are numerous ways in which phenomena can be sorted, and the idea of the "one and only right and real" classification system is (at least in most research areas) merely an idealization" (p. 19). The basic idea is that the abstract (boundary) object for classification can be described at different grains of analysis, within and across the components of the agent-action-context sequence. This feature creates flexibility in the development and coordination of differing classification systems and can incorporate distinct systems while assuming that there is only one object subject to classification. For example, sexual offending can be categorized in terms of psychological deficits (agents and contexts), offence pathways or trajectories (actions), and crime scene factors (contexts). Each of these different classification systems can be linked to the abstract boundary object of sexual offending, with its three core components.

Of course, classification of offending is a more basic conceptual task than explanation; it provides targets for explanatory theories. Our idea is to draw from this concept so that DRF are viewed as boundary objects rather than simply summaries of different sets of factors. Thus, it directs attention to a single object with three components to it: agent-action-context. Each of these can then become a focus of both descriptive and explanatory work by researchers. The three components of DRF boundary objects with their convergence on agents and actions, are equivalent to the major features of explanatory models such as the PAM. In a way, the concept boundary objects makes it much easier to translate DRF into aspects of agency.

3.6 Summary: Reformulating DRF

Despite these suggestions for advancing our understanding of DRF, progress has been limited. We suggest that the crucial task of adding depth to explanations of offending has been impeded by a number of factors. The first is a lack of understanding of theoretical research methods. These are not routinely the focus of psychology courses and they are often overlooked at the expense of experimental or descriptive research designs. There appears to be a failure to understand that the field will not progress unless attention is paid to conceptual issues. The second (related) potential barrier is the lack of consensus on how these factors should be conceptualized and measured. This has a clear impact on the ability of theoretical researchers to draw information from empirical studies and limits the availability of data for conceptual analysis. The third, and perhaps most serious barrier is the widespread reliance upon statistical relationships as explanations which can guide practice. A lack of critical attention to the assumptions underpinning the dominant approach will likely lead to an acceptance of the status quo and a theoretical dead end. In order to overcome this impasse and in line with the suggestions outlined above, in the following chapter we will briefly sketch out a methodological framework and point to areas for further development. This approach can work in tandem with the suggestion that DRF are conceptualized as boundary objects. However, we will not provide any specific local theories here; this is a substantial task beyond the scope of this book.

References

Andrews, D. A., & Bonta, J. (2010). *The psychology of criminal conduct* (5th ed.). New Providence, NJ: LexisNexis.

Baird, C. (2009). *A question of evidence: A critique of risk assessment models used in the justice system*. Madison, WI: National Council on Crime & Delinquency.

Baker, L. R. (2015). Human persons as social entities. *Journal of Social Ontology, 1*, 77–87. https://doi.org/10.1515/jso-2014-0037
Bowker, G. C., Timmermans, S., Clarke, A. E., & Balka, E. (Eds.). (2015). *Boundary objects and beyond: Working with Leigh Star*. Boston, MA: MIT. Kindle Edition.
Bradford-Hill, A. (1965). The environment of disease: Association or causation? *Proceedings of the Royal Society of Medicine, 58*, 295–300.
Carter, E., Ward, T., & Hughes, A. (in press). The classification of crime and its related problems: A pluralistic approach. *Aggression and Violent Behavior.* https://doi.org/10.1016/j.avb.2020.101440.
Cuthbert, B. N., & Kozak, M. J. (2013). Constructing constructs for psychopathology: The NIMH research domain criteria. *Journal of Abnormal Psychology, 122*(3), 928–937. https://doi.org/10.1037/a0034028
Lilienfeld, S. O. (2014). The research domain criteria (RDoC): An analysis of methodological and conceptual challenges. *Behaviour Research and Therapy, 62*, 129–139. https://doi.org/10.1016/j.brat.2014.07.019
Magnus, P. D. (2012). *Scientific inquiry and natural kinds: From planets to mallards*. Basingstoke, UK: Palgrave Macmillan.
Mann, R. E., Hanson, R. K., & Thornton, D. (2010). Assessing risk for sexual recidivism: Some proposals on the nature of psychologically meaningful risk factors. *Sexual Abuse, 22*(2), 191–217. https://doi.org/10.1177/1079063210366039
Mitchell, S. D. (2003). *Biological complexity and integrative pluralism*. Cambridge, UK: Cambridge University Press.
Murphy, D. (2016). Validity, realism, and normativity. In P. Zachar, D. S. Stoyanov, M. Aragona, & A. Jablensky (Eds.), *Alternative perspectives on psychiatric validation* (pp. 60–75). Oxford, UK: Oxford University Press.
Schmidt, S., Heffernan, R., & Ward, T. (2020). Why we cannot explain cross-cultural differences in risk assessment. *Aggression and Violent Behavior, 50*, 1–12. https://doi.org/10.1016/j.avb.2019.101346
Shepherd, S. M., & Lewis-Fernandez, R. (2016). Forensic risk assessment and cultural diversity: Contemporary challenges and future directions. *Psychology, Public Policy, and Law, 22*(4), 427. https://doi.org/10.1037/law0000102
Star, S. L., & Griesemer, J. R. (1989). Institutional ecology, 'translations' and boundary objects: Amateurs and professionals in Berkeley's Museum of Vertebrate Zoology, 1907–39. *Social Studies of Science, 19*, 387–420.
Ward, T. (2014). The explanation of sexual offending: From single factor theories to integrative pluralism. *Journal of Sexual Aggression, 20*(2), 130–141. https://doi.org/10.1080/13552600.2013.870242
Ward, T. (2016). Dynamic risk factors: Scientific kinds or predictive constructs. *Psychology, Crime & Law, 22*(1–2), 2–16. https://doi.org/10.1080/1068316x.2015.1109094
Ward, T. (2019). Why theory matters in correctional psychology. *Aggression and Violent Behavior, 48*, 36–45. https://doi.org/10.1016/j.avb.2019.08.015
Ward, T., & Carter, E. (2019). The classification of offending and crime related problems: A functional perspective. *Psychology, Crime & Law, 25*(6), 542–560. https://doi.org/10.1080/1068316X.2018.1557182
Ward, T., Durrant, R., & Dixon, L. (in press, a). The classification of crime: Towards pluralism: *Aggression and Violent Behavior.* https://doi.org/10.1016/j.avb.2020.101474
Ward, T., Durrant, R., & Dixon, L. (Eds.). (in press, b). Classification of crime: Issues in theory, research and practice. Special issue of Aggression and Violent Behavior.
Ward, T., & Fortune, C.-A. (2016). From dynamic risk factors to causal processes: A methodological framework. *Psychology, Crime & Law, 22*(1–2), 190–202. https://doi.org/10.1080/1068316x.2015.1117080
Ward, T., & Heffernan, R. (2017). The role of values in forensic and correctional rehabilitation. *Aggression and Violent Behavior, 37*, 42–51. https://doi.org/10.1016/j.avb.2017.09.002

Chapter 4
Reformulating Dynamic Risk Factors and Practice Implications

Abstract The field has reached a point where Dynamic Risk Factors (DRF) are no longer adequate explanations for offending, we need more comprehensive and mechanistic explanations of behavior to guide individual case formulations and treatment. In this chapter we first briefly outline a unique conceptual framework to guide researchers in constructing general explanatory theories of offending. While this is a framework for research, it has practical implications for the treatment of individuals who have committed offences. We suggest that its main application at this stage is in the formulation of individual cases, as it can guide practitioners' reasoning about the different capacities and mechanisms which may be relevant to behavior and thus behavior change. We discuss the implications of this in terms of current approaches to rehabilitation.

Keywords Dynamic risk factors · Causal mechanisms

The usability and utility of theory in practice should be of key concern to researchers. While it may be satisfying and valuable to develop a coherent and comprehensive explanation for certain phenomena, ethical concerns dictate that researchers should also consider the practical implications of their work. At this point we would like to point out that despite some promising findings, the current state of correctional intervention is lacking and suggest that we need to do better. As summarized by Hough (2010):

> The most consistent finding to emerge from those examining programmes for reducing offending is that insufficient research has been conducted of high enough quality to say much with any confidence. The second most consistent finding… is that knowledge about what works is inconsistent and incomplete. The third finding that consistently emerges is that some programmes sometimes work. Those that have emerged as successful most frequently are cognitive behavioural programmes. This probably reflects the fact that they

R. Heffernan, T. Ward, *Dynamic Risk Factors for Sexual Offending: Causal Considerations*, SpringerBriefs in Psychology,
https://doi.org/10.1007/978-3-030-58275-3_4

> have been developed on a firm theoretical foundation—but also that in their nature, they are amenable to evaluation. (p. 13)

We suggest that at least some of this inconsistency is due to confusion surrounding its foundational constructs, DRF. In line with the need principle (Andrews & Bonta, 2010), DRF are the targets of effective interventions. They guide tasks such as intervention assessments and case formulation, treatment planning and goal setting, developing program manuals, and the measurement of progress. Throughout these tasks, theories are used by practitioners to understand their clients' presenting problems and work with them to facilitate change and observe progress against areas of need (Ward, 2019; Ward, Polaschek, & Beech, 2006). Without a coherent understanding of what DRF are, how they relate to offending, and how they might change, practitioners are limited in their ability to promote change and reduce harm.

This chapter will first outline a framework for research into the mechanisms underpinning DRF. We will then explore what could change at present to both acknowledge the limitations of our understanding of the causes of offending and capitalize on what is known about human behavior. While significant theoretical work remains, there are implications for viewing DRF (and offending) as boundary objects (i.e., aspects of agency capacities, goal-directed actions, and normative contexts). We will first outline the methodological framework which we suggest has merit in moving the field closer to providing mechanistic explanations for offending. Following this, we will outline current approaches to correctional treatment and discuss how these align with a view of persons as agents who engage in goal-directed behaviors. Finally, we will make some suggestions for how practice might look moving forward, building upon the reformulation of DRF put forward in this book and future research into the composition of DRF.

4.1 Risk-Causality Method

The Risk-Causality Method was introduced by Heffernan, Ward, Vandevelde, and Van Damme (2019) to address the conceptual problems with DRF and develop more comprehensive explanations of offending (see Fig. 4.1). It consists of three phases which draw from the suggestions discussed in the previous chapter. The first task for researchers is to identify candidate DRF for reformulation, it is suggested that at a minimum these should have a strong statistical relationship with offending and be able to be considered plausible causes of behavior (i.e., psychologically meaningful risk factors). Mann, Hanson, and Thornton's (2010) meta-analysis contains a comprehensive list for sexual offending (e.g., intimacy deficits, emotional congruence with children, self-regulation problems). These factors should then be used to construct an exemplar of an individual who experiences each problem and engages in sexual offending (i.e., a description of the DRF and offence co-existing). This should be repeated for multiple DRF, their relationship with offending is the target for explanation. In the first phase of the RCM researchers should take these exemplars and deconstruct them into their behavioral or mental state aspects (i.e., symptom-like descriptions; agency features), contextual features, and potentially causal elements (i.e., agency features; actions). The result of this phase will be a set of potential causal processes. In the second phase these potential causal processes should be investigated across multiple levels of analysis, including biological (including physiological and neurological), phenomenological (i.e., psychological states and processes), behavioral (i.e., actions related to these processes), and contextual (i.e., interpersonal/cultural and environmental influences on these processes). The result of these analyses will be a set of local models for each potential causal process. In the third and final phase of the RCM, researchers should utilize integrative pluralism to link these local models with each other and patterns of behavior (e.g., offending). They may do this by locating them within a theory of agency or goal-directed behavior (e.g., the PAM discussed earlier).

It goes without saying that this is no easy feat, it has taken the field decades of research to get to where we currently are, and this involves a substantial shift in the way research is conducted. It also draws from a range of research disciplines and methods and will require collaborative research practices; it is unlikely that any one researcher could provide all of the data and local theories necessary for this framework. Thus, it requires inter-field co-ordination and an important prerequisite for this to occur is construct validity and equivalence (Sullivan, 2019). That is, researchers need to make sure that they are working with the same theoretical conception of DRF and agree on ways of measuring them. This research will fail if researchers cannot settle on consistent definitions and descriptions of key phenomena of interest. Therefore, the first step is to clearly define the concepts and relationships which are of interest, thus providing an initial set of exemplars. It is likely that these will be expanded upon across time, for example, in relation to new discoveries or other theoretical developments. However, having a clear starting point will ensure that researchers are investigating the same things. Researchers may then choose to focus

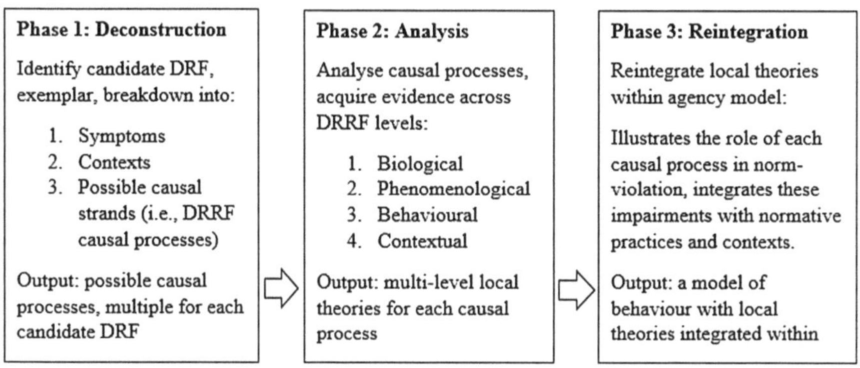

Fig. 4.1 The risk-causality method. Reprinted from "Dynamic risk factors and explanation: The risk-causality method," by R. Heffernan, T. Ward, S. Vandevelde, and L. Van Damme, 2019, *Aggression and Violent Behavior, 44*, p. 53. Copyright 2018 by Elsevier Ltd. Reprinted with permission

on a particular area of interest and use their expertise to provide local theories to be integrated with others in a comprehensive, multi-level explanation of behavior. Each local theory which adds to this body of research is like a tile in a mosaic, each contributing to a larger picture of the causal mechanisms underpinning behaviors, including offending and other norm violations.

To illustrate, researchers may decide to create a set of local theories depicting the possible causal processes underpinning *emotional congruence with children*. Candidate causal processes include: threat detection systems (i.e., fearful of adults/ women), viewing children as sources of reward/pleasure, attentional biases towards signs of affection from children, theory of mind impairments, and so on. Different researchers may develop local theories based on what is currently known about impairments in these systems and the way they ought to function, these should span multiple levels of explanation. Local theories depicting potential causal processes may then be integrated within a theory of agency such as the PAM, this final step can facilitate an understanding of how these factors might interact and be proximally linked with behavior. Figure 4.2 contains an example of how emotional congruence and threat detection mechanisms may be integrated within the PAM. As further local theories are developed, they can be integrated and linked together to explain why an individual might experience emotional congruence with children and how that might lead to offending.

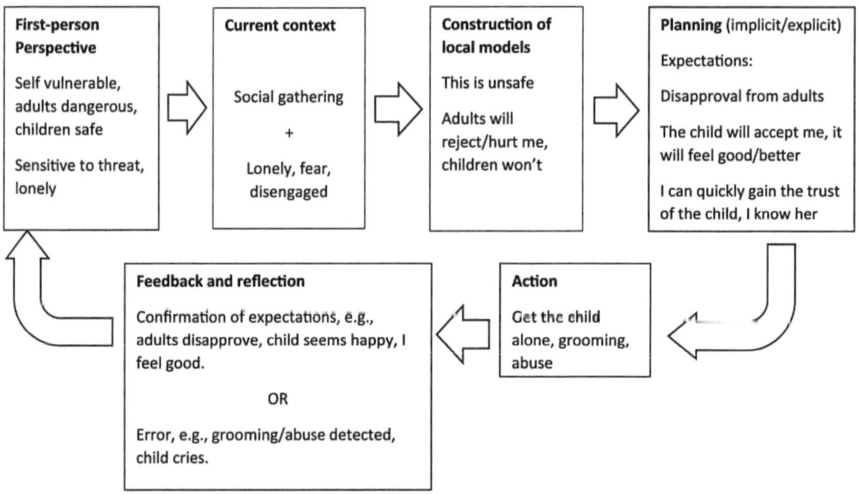

Fig. 4.2 The risk-causality method, example of threat detection and emotional congruence with children integrated within the predictive agency model. Reprinted from "Dynamic risk factors and explanation: The risk-causality method," by R. Heffernan, T. Ward, S. Vandevelde, and L. Van Damme, 2019, *Aggression and Violent Behavior, 44*, p. 53. Copyright 2018 by Elsevier Ltd. Reprinted with permission

4.2 Implications: Rehabilitation Theories

In the remainder of this chapter we will outline some preliminary implications of the RCM in practice, however, it is first necessary to explore in greater depth what the field of rehabilitation or treatment currently looks like. As discussed earlier, rehabilitation frameworks contain (1) overarching values, principles, and aims, (2) assumptions about the causes offending and behavioral change, and (3) practice guidelines, principles, and tools for use in interventions (Ward, Melser, & Yates, 2007). For example, the purpose of using the RNR model is to reduce victimization (reflecting social and ethical values) by taking a 'rational empirical' approach to research (reflecting epistemic values); it contains general principles (i.e., RNR), is based on a *general personality and cognitive social learning* view of persons and the assumption that DRF cause offending, and contains additional principles and risk assessment tools to guide practice. The RNR model proposes that effective intervention occurs via change in criminogenic factors through collaborative, compassionate, and dignified human service (Polaschek, 2012). However, in practice responsivity to the individual and their unique needs is often overlooked (Polaschek, 2012). Needs which are not empirically linked with reoffending are largely seen as a responsivity issue—they may be targeted if they are barriers to treatment. The Good Lives Model (GLM; Ward & Maruna, 2007) augments the RNR by providing an approach to treatment, rather than a set of guidelines for correctional practice generally. It offers a strength-based view of persons and views offending behavior as motivated by normative human needs. This is compatible with the RNR, as it also views risk reduction as a core goal; it simply disagrees that an exclusive focus on DRF is the best way to achieve this.

4.3 The Risk-Need-Responsivity Model

As the RNR model was outlined earlier in this book, we will only briefly repeat the core principles here. The *risk principle* states that individuals at higher risk of reoffending will benefit most from more intensive intervention and that lower risk clients should receive less intervention. The *need principle* proposes that changeable features reliably associated with reductions in recidivism (i.e., DRF or criminogenic needs) should be targeted in treatment programs relative to those that have no demonstrated empirical relationship to crime. The *responsivity principle* states that correctional programs should use empirically supported treatment models (e.g., cognitive behavioral therapy) and be responsive to individual characteristics such as learning style and level of motivation. The first two principles (risk and need) are used to select treatment intensity and targets (based on DRF), and the whole set of principles are employed to guide the way practice is implemented.

We have concerns with this model which stem from its prioritization of prediction over explanation and its tendency to rely heavily on inconsistent evidence which does not adequately support its assumptions about the causes of offending. In terms of its core principles, these issues mainly impact upon the *need* and *responsivity* principles. The need principle is based on statistical evidence concerning the best predictors of recidivism and assumptions about the (possible) causal nature of DRF. As argued throughout this book, DRF in their current state cannot be considered causes of crime. The general responsivity principle requires that practitioners and program designers are responsive to what works, and we suggest that we need to look beyond treatment outcome and studies and variation in DRF and recidivism rates in order to understand whether and why certain types of treatment are successful. Finally, the specific responsivity principle requires that practitioners be responsive to the needs of individuals. We argue that this requires both research into individuals' experiences of change and rehabilitation, as well as a comprehensive understanding of human functioning and agency. We will now explore each of these issues in more detail.

Programs adhering to the RNR principles have demonstrated *relative* success (compared to those which do not) in reducing recidivism rates (Andrews & Bonta, 2010; Bonta & Andrews, 2017; Dowden & Andrews, 2000; Gannon, Olver, Mallion, & James, 2019; Hanson, Bourgon, Helmus, & Hodgson, 2009) and so long as this continues, they should be used to guide practice. For example, Hanson et al. (2009) reported 10.9 per cent sexual and 31.8 per cent general recidivism following treatment for sexual offending (versus 19.2 and 48.3 per cent in the untreated group, respectively) and found that programmes adhering to the RNR principles had greater reductions than those which did not. The body of work which supports these principles is currently the most robust evidence available to guide practice, and we are not suggesting that we abandon all we currently know about what works. However, as pointed out in chapter two, the evidence supporting the need principle is currently inconclusive. Treatment resulting in changes to DRF is not consistently linked with reductions in reoffending. Further, statistical associations between exposure to intervention and rates of recidivism offer a general (but imperfect) answer to the question of whether treatment 'works', but these research designs cannot tell us whether and how or why people have made enduring changes to their lives. Some limitations with treatment outcome studies were briefly mentioned in chapter two, these include various methodological weaknesses, the subjectivity of risk ratings and reliance on self-report data, the composite and eclectic nature of treatment programmes, and the use of recidivism as an outcome measure (see Heffernan, Wegerhoff, & Ward, 2019).

We argue that these studies offer a rather narrow view of the available knowledge concerning rehabilitation, desistance, and change, and suggest a broader interpretation of what constitutes evidence and success. There are three reasons for this stance: (1) recidivism is a difficult to measure and decontextualized outcome variable (Jung & Gulayets, 2011), (2) the evidence concerning criminal behavior ought to be drawn from multiple disciplines and inform explanations of individual functioning rather than relying upon lists of correlates (Heffernan, Ward, et al., 2019), and (3) the success of current rehabilitation programs has not yet been satisfactorily proven and we must consider new ways to increase their effectiveness. Knowledge is cumulative, rather than one definitive study proving that treatment is effective or ineffective, and our understanding of its effects will grow through the accumulation of many smaller studies using various methods (Collaborative Outcome Data Committee, 2007). In relation to this issue, Farrall (2005) makes the point that:

> … without a willingness at least to consider in-depth the experiences of individuals who have successfully negotiated the transitions from "offender", it is unlikely that efforts to encourage desistence (e.g., the What Works movement) will produce the sorts of results so desperately needed. (p. 383)

This mainly relates to the general responsivity principle (i.e., how we should go about treatment in an evidence-based way), but also has implications for the other principles. In order to be truly responsive to the evidence concerning what works, we must broaden the scope of the research relied upon to inform intervention design (i.e., general responsivity) and delivery (i.e., specific responsivity). This means paying attention to qualitative research and listening to program participants' perceptions about what they need in order to change. It also means developing an understanding of offending which is not based solely on the correlates of crime. By focusing on the way systems ought to function in order to meet certain needs or perform certain tasks, researchers have a better chance of determining what has gone wrong when these processes lead to offending.

The analysis of DRF provided throughout this book has seriously called into question the legitimacy of relying upon these concepts as explanations for offending and targets of interventions. This is the basis of the need principle, so we suggest that this principle is either fundamentally flawed or at best under-developed. Further, given the reliance of the other RNR principles on the concept of DRF, the theoretical basis of the whole model is arguably undermined. It is likely that the domains of functioning and arenas of life reflected within DRF categories are in 'need' of prosocial change (i.e., in order to reduce harm), or that when psychological change occurs, we will also see changes in these areas (i.e., they are indicators of a criminal or prosocial life orientation). However, without an understanding of *what* needs to change and *how* this might happen, we are unable to adequately plan and deliver treatment or monitor its success. Useful case formulation requires that practitioners understand the probable *causes* of the problems reflected within criminal lifestyles and patterns of behavior. In addition, it is worth considering that the factors which reduce crime may be different to those which have been shown to precede offending (Kroner, Polaschek, Serin, & Skeem, 2017; Polaschek, 2016; Serin & Lloyd, 2009). In other words, even if we understand the causes of offending, we may then need to also look to the causes of desistance in order to understand and influence the change process (see Laws & Ward, 2011). One potential way to address this issue is to adopt a more holistic view of persons as goal-directed agents motivated by universal needs.

4.4 The Good Lives Model

As discussed, the GLM broadens the focus of rehabilitation from simply the reduction of risk to also providing participants with the resources required to live a good life. We will now outline the GLM in more detail, as it provides a treatment approach which we will build upon with our suggestions for practice. The reason for this focus on the GLM is that it augments the RNR model by providing a motivating and personally meaningful approach to therapy that fits well with an agency perspective of human behavior. The approach to DRF developed throughout this book is consistent with the GLM, and future research in line with the RCM will add depth to the model by specifying the mechanisms underpinning DRF. Following our description of the GLM and the contributions of this approach, we will describe this addition in more depth.

As discussed above, the GLM's view of persons is as goal-directed beings who are motivated to engage with their environments in order to pursue a range of valued outcomes, termed 'primary human goods' (PHG). The PHG contained within the GLM have varied slightly over time, a recent list includes excellence in work, excellence in play, creativity, knowledge, relatedness, community, pleasure, life, inner peace, spirituality, and excellence in agency (Purvis & Ward, 2020). The means (i.e., behaviors, strategies, outcomes) which persons use to meet these needs are termed 'secondary human goods'. For example, one person may meet their need for 'inner peace' (i.e., freedom from emotional distress) through regular exercise or therapy, while another may use substances or violence to deal with emotions. The purpose of treatment according to the GLM is twofold; to prevent potential harm to victims (i.e., reduce reoffending) and provide the individual with the internal and external resources required to live a personally fulfilling good life. Proponents of the GLM suggest that these two aims are not mutually exclusive, as criminal behavior is seen as a consequence of problems within an individual's (largely implicit) 'good life plan' (GLP). This plan contains both primary and secondary goods, PHG are prioritized to different degrees across individuals and situations, and the secondary goods used depend on both opportunities available and individual capacities. Thus, according to the GLM, the causes or contributors to offending and related problems (i.e., DRF) are deficits or barriers in the internal and external resources needed to achieve PHG in ways which do not harm others. These problems should be the focus of treatment; interventions aim to build strengths in these resources in order to meet the dual aims of risk reduction and good life promotion.

According to Ward and colleagues (Ward, 2002a, 2002b; Ward & Fisher, 2005; Ward, Mann, & Gannon, 2007) there are four types of problem which can arise and often interact or co-exist within GLP: capacity, means, conflict, and scope. In brief, when *capacities* or resources (internal and external) are lacking, an individual may turn to antisocial behaviors (i.e., harmful *means*), such as offending, in order to attain PHG. Sometimes problematic actions and their outcomes can *conflict* with an individual's attainment of other goods. For example, poor coping abilities or lack of problem-solving skills (capacity) may lead to use of violence (means) aimed at attaining excellence in agency or control, which may result in imprisonment and obstruct an individual's ability to meet needs such as relatedness or pleasure (conflict). The final problem, lack of *scope,* occurs when certain goods are prioritized at the expense of others, and not all are represented within a person's GLP. In addition, GLM researchers have expanded upon these four problems to empirically identify and describe two routes to offending, *direct* and *indirect* (Purvis, Ward, & Willis, 2011). The direct route occurs when an individual's capacities and resources are lacking, and offending is used as a means to attain PHG. The indirect route involves conflict or problems with scope, and offending occurs as a result of other unhelpful behaviors rather than being directly used to meet needs.

GLM interventions are based upon a participant's personally meaningful GLP and aim to develop the internal and external resources required to meet needs without harming others. The GLP contains all PHG categories to varying degrees (chosen by the individual) and the secondary goods (both goals and strategies) required to attain these in healthy and prosocial ways. It is important that the dual focus on reduced risk and good lives is evident throughout assessment and treatment. For example, these two priorities can be linked by identifying which PHG may have been related to offending (directly or indirectly) and exploring these relationships—for example, are there problems with capacities, means, conflict, or scope? Many of the problems identified are likely to correspond to established DRF categories, for example, capacities such as problem solving, emotional-coping, and/or perspective-taking may be lacking. Treatment goals will include strengthening these capacities (internal resources) so the individual can meet their needs without relying upon harmful means. In addition, external resources and conditions (i.e., opportunities and constraints) can support or obstruct goods attainment, and so these should also be included in a comprehensive GLP. There is a dual focus on promoting PHG and overcoming barriers (i.e., criminogenic needs, problems within past GLP), this is achieved through collaboration and a focus on individual goals, rather than simply avoiding risk.

The GLM is a strengths-based approach to correctional rehabilitation because it is responsive to people's particular interests, abilities, and aspirations (Ward & Maruna, 2007). It also asks practitioners to explicitly construct intervention plans that help people acquire the capabilities to achieve personally meaningful goals. Rehabilitation plans should aim to equip persons with the knowledge, skills, opportunities, and resources necessary to satisfy their needs in ways that do not harm others. Related to its strong focus on persons' core commitments and lifestyles that reflect these, there is a corresponding stress on agency. Because of the assumption that individuals who commit crimes, like the rest of us, actively seek to satisfy their needs through whatever means are available to them, any rehabilitation plan should be pitched at the level of agency, goals, planning, and environments. The GLM is an ecological model which acknowledges the relationship between the environments in which persons live and the capabilities and resources they need to live meaningful and crime free lives (Ward & Stewart, 2003). Criminogenic needs or DRF are conceptualised within the GLM as internal or external obstacles (i.e., flaws within a good life plan) that make it difficult for individuals to secure primary goods in personally meaningful and socially acceptable ways.

Proponents of the GLM have developed guidelines and practice tools to aid in the integration of the model into programs (e.g., Purvis et al., 2011; Willis, Yates, Gannon, & Ward, 2013; Yates, Prescott, & Ward, 2010). It should be used throughout the tasks of assessment and case formulation, case management and intervention planning, development of program manuals, and establishing the therapeutic relationship. The GLM is used internationally, including in New Zealand (Whitehead, Ward, & Collie, 2007), Australia (Willis & Ward, 2013), the United Kingdom (Langlands, Ward, & Gilchrist, 2009), Belgium (Van Damme, Hoeve, Vermeiren, Vanderplasschen, & Colins, 2016), Singapore (Chu, Koh, Zeng, & Teoh, 2015), the United States (Willis, Ward, & Levenson, 2014), and Canada (Marshall, Marshall, Serran, & O'Brien, 2011). It has been suggested as appropriate for use with a range of participants, including youth (Fortune, 2017; Wainwright & Nee, 2014; Wylie & Griffin, 2013), female (Van Damme et al., 2016), elderly (Di Lorito, Völlm, & Dening, 2018), intellectually disabled (Aust, 2010), mentally disordered (Barnao, Ward, & Casey, 2015, 2016; Gannon, King, Miles, Lockerbie, & Willis, 2011), and non-Western (Chu et al., 2015; Leaming & Willis, 2016) offending populations. In addition, beyond its preliminary use in interventions for sexual offending it has been considered useful for the treatment of substance abuse (Thakker & Ward, 2010), violence (Whitehead et al., 2007), domestic violence (Langlands et al., 2009), and residential burglary (Taylor, 2017).

In terms of its role in these programmes, it is often viewed as an 'add-on' to traditional risk focused interventions, rather than being used as intended to guide the entirety of treatment. For example, Willis et al. (2014) evaluated the operationalization of the GLM in North American programs and found that it was most often used within program delivery (i.e., developing positive therapist characteristics) and as an additional component to treatment (e.g., self-management plans at program completion). These authors proposed that "enhancing program consistency with the GLM requires using it as a comprehensive theoretical framework to guide interventions throughout the entirety of a program" (Willis et al., 2014, p. 77). Thus, while the GLM is utilised internationally, there are issues with its implementation and inconsistencies with its intended role throughout the rehabilitation process.

4.5 Reformulated DRF and Case Formulation

We will now offer some suggestions concerning how the RCM may influence the crucial task of case formulation. The reconceptualization of DRF advocated for throughout this book is essentially in line with the GLM concepts of internal (and external) resources and obstacles. They are symptomatic of agency capacities and contexts that either facilitate or obstruct goal-directed behavior, and thus direct persons towards or away from antisocial, harmful, or maladaptive outcomes. Future research in line with the RCM can add depth to the GLM by pointing to more specific areas where weakness may be present. Even at this preliminary point in the reconceptualization of DRF, practitioners may find these ideas useful to guide the assessment and treatment of individuals who have committed offences. Simply relying on existing case formulation models or etiological theories that assume that DRF (as currently described in the literature) are possible causes is likely to result in overly general, poorly integrated formulations (i.e., everyone looks the same or possible hypotheses are overlooked). Our suggestion is that in the domain of intervention DRF should only be used to indicate *general problem areas* and be regarded as summaries of possible causes (i.e., agency or personal factors), behaviors, and contextual factors. The concept of boundary objects helps with this task by virtue of its focus on a common object that can then be unpacked into subcomponents relating to problems with agency, action, and contexts. By the processes of deconstruction, analysis, and reintegration (i.e., the RCM) we can put DRF to work in ways that are likely to give us a deeper understanding of why and how individuals act in ways that harm other people.

Case formulation is the analogue of theory construction in the practice domain; the creation of an individualized explanatory model that accounts for the onset, interrelationships, and maintenance of problems associated with crime (Hart & Logan, 2011; Sturmey & McMurran, 2011; Ward & Beech, 2015). Forensic case formulation is used to guide the rehabilitation of those who have committed offences, and until recently has received relatively little attention in the literature (Sturmey & McMurran, 2011). It is an important task, which involves the gathering of risk-related data and construction of a plausible explanation (i.e., a hypothesis) for how and why particular factors cause and maintain offending. Typically, it is based upon the widely accepted 'propensity model' of risk, where a number of long-term vulnerabilities (i.e., DRF) interact with environmental triggers and opportunities to influence behavior (Beech & Ward, 2004). Case formulation is generally guided by practitioners' training in cognitive behavioral theory (i.e., CBT) and a general personality and cognitive social learning perspective of persons (i.e., the GPCSL perspective). There is an emphasis on faulty thinking, offence-supportive core beliefs, antisocial traits, and learned behavior. In the sense that it links DRF with behavior, case formulation aims to bridge the gap between prediction and explanation. It guides practice via the integration of empirical knowledge and theoretical understanding of DRF. The problem currently facing forensic and correctional practitioners is that existing case formulation approaches assume that DRF are theoretically coherent constructs (see Sturmey & McMurran, 2011), however, as argued throughout this book, they are not.

The purpose of case formulation is to identify factors which are relevant for the *individual,* and to use these to generate predictions for future behavior and targets for intervention (Hart, Sturmey, Logan, & McMurran, 2011). Hart et al. (2011) provide a number of useful suggestions and evaluation criteria for forensic case formulation. Firstly, it is important that case formulations provide coherent narratives which are simple in that they avoid the incorporation of unnecessary data and assumptions, and diachronic in that they span the past, present, and future rather than being fixated upon the past (Hart et al., 2011). Another important consideration is the explanatory breadth of a formulation, for example, the extent to which it accounts for critical evidence and ties all relevant information together. It must be internally coherent, consistent, and contain assumptions which are compatible (i.e., do not contradict each other). Another criterion worth noting is a formulation's acceptability; whether it is useful and comprehensible for the individual for whom it was created (i.e., consistent with common-sense explanations rather than just complex scientific theory).

While forensic case formulation should be individualized in order to tailor treatment, in practice the hypotheses and goals formed often center upon correlates of recidivism at the aggregate level (i.e., the need principle). This is particularly the case when assessments are undertaken by paraprofessionals (i.e., not qualified psychologists). This can result in case formulations and treatment plans which look remarkably similar across individuals; they lack explanatory depth and relevance because they rely upon descriptions of vague and composite constructs. Practitioners are often provided with a structured interview template containing a list of DRF deemed relevant for the individual if they feature in their offending. These are then translated into goals for treatment. For example, challenging and replacing attitudes concerning sex and violence, abstaining from or reducing substance use, improving emotion management, developing problem-solving skills, and so on. It is expected that these correlates cause (or at least contribute to) individual offending, and therefore that reducing or removing their influence will reduce the likelihood of reoffending. However, the empirical findings concerning the links between improvement on DRF and subsequent changes in offending behavior are currently mixed (Duwe & Rocque, 2016; Heffernan, Wegerhoff, et al., 2019; Serin, Lloyd, Helmus, Derkzen, & Luong, 2013), there are concerns about construct validity (Cording, Beggs Christofferson, & Grace, 2016; Polaschek, 2016), and there is little understanding of the mechanisms underlying the change process.

Hart et al. (2011) suggest that forensic case-formulation should be *inferential*, involving abductive reasoning from data to phenomena and causal mechanisms, and *ampliative* in generating new knowledge rather than merely re-describing problems. Therefore, the development of mechanistic explanations is directly relevant to forensic practice, both in helping to locate the source (i.e., underlying cause) of impairments and also in understanding how these problems have developed over time. *Etiological* explanations focus on the process of an outcome being brought about, and typically refer to events or features which temporally precede an offence (i.e., potential causes). For example, loneliness and intoxication may lead to a sexual offence. *Compositional* explanations on the other hand refer to the structure of phenomena across multiple levels of analysis (Ward, Wilshire, & Jackson, 2018). To illustrate, several recent fMRI studies have reported that individuals with psychopathic traits show reduced neural responses in several key regions when they view stimuli designed to provoke an empathic response (e.g., facial expressions, pictures of bodily injuries; see Marsh et al., 2013). The brain regions implicated include the amygdala and ventral prefrontal regions (e.g., the rostral anterior cingulate cortex and/or the ventromedial prefrontal cortex; see also Blair, 2013). It is tempting to conclude from these studies that psychopathic traits are *caused* by abnormalities within the brain—that they represent a "brain illness". However, such a conclusion is not warranted. These studies merely elucidate the different types of neural patterns that *constitute* what is termed psychopathic functioning and behavior. Indeed, an inability to respond empathically to others forms *part of the definition* of psychopathy. So, it is not at all surprising that this lack of empathy is also evident in neurobiological measures that index a person's emotional response to the suffering of others.

Case formulations typically provide an etiological explanation in the sense that they contain proposed distal and proximal influences upon behavior, and predictions about the sorts of triggers and contexts which are likely to precede any future offences. We propose that these individual etiological explanations will be more useful if they are supplemented by compositional explanations concerning the different phenomena implicated within these narratives. In other words, both are necessary for developing comprehensive explanations. Theories explaining the relationship between DRF and offending and the mechanisms underpinning this relationship are therefore crucial within case formulation, they guide the process of *inference* from *descriptions* of thoughts and behaviors to *explanations* of their possible causes and targets for intervention. As they are partially informed by narrative data (i.e., the person's account of the offence), these explanations can be thought of as comprising first, second, and third person perspectives. While the offence itself is usually not able to be observed by the practitioner or researcher formulating the explanation, they may rely upon the perspectives of the individuals involved (i.e., perpetrator and victim), others present (e.g., witnesses, law enforcement), and others involved in previous assessments (e.g., Corrections/justice staff). In addition, they rely upon empirical data which has identified common areas of difficulty for those who have offended (i.e., DRF), and opinions of their relevance to the individual. These are inferred from the perspectives of the individual themselves, those who know them well, or practitioners who have worked with them previously. Ideally explanations will combine evidence from numerous high-quality sources in order to form a comprehensive and accurate formulation that is guided by a sound theory (or theories) of human functioning (Hart et al., 2011). This would also contribute to a formulation's reliability; the likelihood that others provided with the same information would come to the same conclusions (Hart et al., 2011).

Further, when formulating cases are important to consider the levels of explanation which are most useful for the task at hand. For example, the mechanisms underpinning offending are comprised of genetic, neurobiological, psychological, social/cultural, and ecological systems (Weerasekera, 1996). Persons are comprised of hierarchical systems, with unique properties emerging at each level. This means that explanations pitched at just one level and ignoring others will be impoverished; all will form a piece of the explanatory picture. For example, in explaining a certain norm-violation, it would be a mistake to overlook the importance of the physical and social environment (e.g., laws, norms, opportunities, etc.), the psychological features (e.g., emotion, cognition), or the biological and neurological influences upon cognition and behavior. While one level may not be reduced to another (e.g., anger cannot be fully explained by physiological arousal) a certain level of analysis could be more suited to a particular task. Certain levels are influenced by others in a process of upward (e.g., biological influences on mood) and downward (e.g., environmental stressors influencing thoughts) causation, reflecting both horizontal and vertical interactions (i.e., between mechanisms and across levels of analysis).

We suggest that *first person*, *intentional* (psychological level) explanations are privileged for the purposes of case formulation, and these should focus on descriptions of behavior—what people do or fail to do, and why. While biological and social levels are important, we ultimately need to understand *why the person acted* in ways that harmed others. This means that useful explanations of serious norm violations and their potential causes must refer to mechanisms and offer an explanation which differentiates adaptive or optimum functioning from dysfunction (Ward & Fortune, 2016). Further, these explanations must be able to account for the interaction of mechanisms (within various DRF categories) which result in norm violations, it is not enough to specify the various mechanism components without a satisfactory account of their causal trajectories. In addition, these explanations will contain both factual and normative components. Factual or causal explanations depict the parts and processes of the mechanism/s comprising a phenomenon, the normative component spells out whether or not it is performing according to some set of standards (i.e., functioning spans a continuum). A research framework such as the RCM has the potential to both guide the development of compositional explanations within individual case formulations (i.e., via local models), and also to understand how various mechanisms are linked with each other and behavior through their integration within a model of agency.

4.6 Practical Implications of Reformulating DRF

In order to make these implications more concrete, we will now make some preliminary suggestions concerning how the different phases or tasks of practice can be responsive to the problems with DRF, agency theories (specifically the PAM), the reformulation developed throughout this book, and future research in line with the RCM. First, as they are based on DRF, existing risk assessments may provide the practitioner with guidance on problem areas to be explored. However, it is important not to jump to conclusions about the causes of behavior or to rely solely on DRF identified through risk assessments to guide case formulation. Rather, practitioners can use these ratings as one source of information (i.e., as potential barriers to prosocial agency), and later check whether the DRF identified via risk assessment are likely to be linked with or addressed within their case formulation. The most important source of information for constructing the case formulation will be the individual's account of their behavior, including the motivations and values underpinning it and the normative context in which it occurred. In line with the GLM, the key tasks are to determine the individual's good life conception (i.e., priorities for living), view these in light of their offending (e.g., direct or indirect routes, problems evident), and then develop goals which center upon the internal and external resources required to live a good life without hurting others (i.e., a GLP). Future research in line with the RCM will add depth to this process, assisting the practitioner by pointing to possible causes (and how these may interact with other mechanisms) and linking these with problem behaviors.

Initially, the practitioner should conduct an exploratory, collaborative, and semi-structured interview to draw out the different components of the GLP. This may be guided by the PAM or a similar model of goal-directed behavior. For example, the practitioner will consider the person's background, early experiences, and how these have shaped identity, interpersonal style, and world view. They will explore the individual's priorities, how they conceptualize a good life and how they have in the past strived to reach this, which may relate to offending. Thus, this initial stage introduces a dual focus on individual well-being and risk. The practitioner will consider emotional functioning, the role of emotion in motivating behavior within certain contexts and explore situation specific representations of the offending context. This will lead into a discussion of the planning phase, considering the expectations which (implicitly or explicitly) influenced the choice of secondary goods. The individual can then describe the behavior and its immediate consequences, including responses from others, and their initial thoughts and emotions. This will help to understand how the behavior fits with their implicit GLP, for example whether and how the behavior was rewarding (i.e., was it successful in meeting needs?), and if it was congruent with expectations. These sources of internal and external feedback can then be discussed, and their impact on general models explored.

When it comes to setting goals and delivering interventions, practitioners can use comprehensive case formulations to develop goals based on the specific causes identified (i.e., hypothesized areas of vulnerability) and the individual's GLP. They can locate the potential sources of problems and then draw from available compositional (i.e., local) models to increase specificity and understanding. This step may involve additional levels of explanation—including social, contextual, and behavioral, as well as sub-personal mechanisms (which levels are relevant will depend on the problem and task at hand). The strategies for developing strengths or resources will vary. For example, vulnerabilities in the planning stage may be addressed by increasing options for action selection (i.e., enhancing problem-solving skills), and problems with general models may be addressed by shifting these to more healthy, adaptive, or prosocial alternatives (i.e., challenging core beliefs). According to the PAM, behavior will change when expectations change, and expectations change via feedback signals. Therefore, rehabilitation should aim to provide learning opportunities or situations where error signals are experienced, so as to alter expectations for future scenarios. For this to happen individuals need to possess the capacities required to learn from these situations, and so this process (i.e., feedback and reflection) may need to be guided and supported by practitioners. It is acknowledged that individuals participating in correctional programs often display problems with self-regulation and planning. However, the majority appear to benefit from training in problem solving and cognitive skills, and therefore clearly possess the basic components of agency. We suggest that with support capacities can be built which allow the individual to explicitly identify and implement alternative strategies (i.e., new secondary goods), and that with practice (and reward) these may become part of their implicit GLP. Thus, this approach advocates for a focus on building capacities and resources (internal and external), including shifting the way the individual represents themselves, others, and the world, in order to support needs attainment and their conception of a good life.

There are existing treatment approaches which are compatible with a focus on agency and its view of feedback and reflection as crucial in changing, updating, or shifting the general models which guide behavior. Correctional treatment generally takes the form of group-based cognitive behavioral interventions, with a focus on patterns of past offending (e.g., developing and analyzing offence maps or offence chains) and safety planning for similar scenarios in the future (i.e., relapse prevention approaches). In this sense, these interventions are already somewhat future-focused, but arguably they could be more so. If we view offending as future-focused rather than driven by past behavior, the emphasis of treatment would be on future outcomes which meet needs without offending (e.g., approach goals within a GLP). Thus, interventions which are consistent with the GLM and its view of persons as goal-directed agents are clearly compatible with the PAM, but so are other widely used techniques.

Seligman, Railton, Baumeister, and Sripada (2016) suggest that CBT can be adapted to be more future-focused, in line with the prospection approach depicted in the PAM. For example, by exploring 'if-then' statements (i.e., causal attributions) or generating alternative simulations of the future and evaluating these. According to Seligman, Railton, Baumeister, and Sripada (2013), there are three key aspects of prospection, the complexity and flexibility of plans, length of the time horizon, and the accuracy of expectations. It is important that individuals are capable of developing multi-faceted options for action (e.g., goals, sub-goals), and that these are flexible to environmental contingencies. In addition, the breadth of options available to a person is important and this relies on the individual's creative capacity as well as past experiences. It is also important that the individual can extend the time horizon of their plans and foreseeable consequences (e.g., long-term thinking). Finally, it is important that expectations are accurate and that individuals are capable of second order desires (e.g., wanting to be motivated towards things).

Key therapist tasks according to this approach include challenging or replacing maladaptive general models, increasing alternative options for planning, strengthening long-term thinking, learning through experience, planning for a better future, increasing incentives for change, and building meaning or purpose (Seligman et al., 2013). The ability to engage in these tasks relies upon a number of capacities, including (but not limited to) creativity and flexibility (e.g., generating alternatives), perspective-taking and other aspects of empathy (e.g., emotion recognition and regulation), self-regulation and delaying gratification, counterfactual and critical thinking, and hope and optimism for the future. There are existing interventions which aim to develop these skills, and we suggest that these will be more effective when underpinned by a comprehensive understanding of human nature and functioning. In addition, an approach to treatment which strengthens an individual's sense of agency or autonomy will lead to a more internal locus of control and experiencing more control over behavior and its outcomes. According to Seligman et al. (2013), when people feel like they have more 'free will' they report engaging in more long-term thinking and conscious deliberation, act in ways that are consistent with their values, and experience more positive outcomes.

In addition, the interactional nature of agency based conceptualizations (e.g., the PAM) is consistent with suggestions that situational and environmental factors be included within intervention and prevention efforts (Smallbone & Cale, 2016). It is important that environments support internal changes through rewarding prosocial behavior (e.g., incentivizing change), and that systemic factors do not get in the way of desistance by obstructing goods attainment (Hannah-Moffat, 2016). Persons need opportunities and reasons to want to change as well as the capacities to do so (i.e., external as well as internal resources). Incentives can be deliberately or professionally provided (e.g., lessening restrictions, work opportunities) and/or naturally occur in environments that reward desistance more than crime. Thus, interventions should explicitly address the reintegration process and develop expectations for this experience which support desistance. For example, encouraging hope and optimism through positive simulations of the future within a GLP, and strengthening skills for creating or seeking out environments which support this.

The compatibility of a stress on agency with these existing approaches is likely a strength, considering the empirical support for the efficacy of CBT in behavioral change generally and with offending populations (Andrews & Bonta, 2010; Bonta & Andrews, 2017). However, focusing on agency-action-contexts expands upon and adds depth to the cognitive behavioral model by spelling out how enduring general models (e.g., 'core beliefs' in CBT) are utilised throughout the agency process, as well as adding to our understanding of the relationship between cognition and emotion. For example, the role of emotion as sense-making and action-guiding is elaborated upon, consistent with emerging research. Our approach is also able to better incorporate the role of motivation and planning within the agency process, and in doing so places autonomy and responsibility for change within the person—as opposed to avoiding or reacting to external sources of risk (i.e., triggers, high risk situations in CBT). In this sense it arguably offers a more sophisticated and comprehensive understanding of cognition and emotion, and the reasons for human behavior.

4.7 Summary: Reformulating DRF and Practice Implications

In summary, it is impossible to construct useful case formulations and treatment plans without having an adequate understanding of the various possible causes of offending and related problems (i.e., DRF). Simply focusing on DRF in the design and delivery of treatment is unlikely to be successful as they fail to reference causal mechanisms; rather they are composite categories containing possible causes (i.e., agency capacities), 'problem' behaviors, and contextual influences. We suggest that DRF should be construed as boundary objects and therefore they are only thinly characterized (i.e., in terms of the *agent-action-context* schema) across different levels of analysis and from different disciplinary perspectives (Ward et al., in press b). The RCM has the potential to guide research and structure case formulation (and more general explanations) which can help practitioners develop deeper mechanistic explanations of individuals' offending and related problems. Understanding that the agent-action-context aspects of DRF can be modelled separately, and at varying levels of analysis, will help researchers to collaborate and link their unique perspectives. We hope that the RCM will begin to bridge the gap between prediction and treatment, and that it will at least alert practitioners to the possibility that there are numerous causal processes underpinning observed problems; DRF are not the end point of inquiry. Ideally this reformulation of DRF will prompt a more individualized and mechanistic approach to case formulation, and a deeper consideration of the assumptions underpinning our explanations of offending.

This chapter has introduced the RCM and explored the implications of the reformulation of DRF for case formulation and treatment in a forensic setting. It loosely sketched out an approach to treatment based on the GLM, agency theories (e.g., the PAM), and future integrated theories (e.g., the RCM). This approach is intended to be complementary to the RNR model, but also to add depth concerning the mechanisms underpinning criminal behavior (i.e., the need principle) and integrate these within a comprehensive model of human behavior which can guide individualized (i.e., responsive) treatment. In this approach DRF are viewed as boundary objects which may indicate areas for further inquiry, and they are likely to demonstrate changes following effective treatment. However, treatment is more broadly focused on strengthening the internal and external resources (i.e., causal processes) required to meet needs in prosocial and healthy ways. The identification of these resources (including the mechanisms which enable them) should be guided by comprehensive theories of human functioning and behavior, such as those arising from the RCM.

The question of what constitutes effective treatment for persons who have committed offences remains, and the evidence used to answer it must come from a range of sources and methods of inquiry. The existing research investigating the use of the RNR and GLM is promising, but it is by no means conclusive, and there are problems with research methods and the implementation of rehabilitation models in practice. For example, many GLM-consistent programs fail to use the model as intended (i.e., to guide the entirety of the program), and the RNR model is routinely reduced to the three core principles and implemented variably internationally (Polaschek, 2012). Future application and evaluation of these models (and agency theories) must integrate them as intended and should evaluate various aspects of treatment and a range of outcomes of interest using multiple methods.

Much is unknown about what is the most effective way to reduce recidivism and we must consider that the current approach may not be adequate (Grady, Edwards Jr, & Pettus-Davis, 2017). The variable and modest effects of interventions suggest that progress is necessary; we should continue to learn from evidence and not shy away from conceptual concerns—both in forensic psychology and other, related disciplines. We suggest that research aiming to advance rehabilitation should not rely solely upon lists of correlates and statistical relationships; the variables involved in the change process are simply too complex. The RNR model has achieved substantial improvements over the years and is based on an impressive amount of evidence, but it is not the final word on what works to reduce recidivism (Fortune & Heffernan, 2019; Newsome & Cullen, 2017; Polaschek, 2012). The RNR principles are based on much of the evidence gathered thus far, but this should encourage critical attention and further development, rather than acceptance of small effect sizes. This is especially important considering the consequences of treatment failure.

References

Andrews, D. A., & Bonta, J. (2010). *The psychology of criminal conduct* (5th ed.). New Providence, NJ: LexisNexis.

Aust, S. (2010). Is the good lives model of offender treatment relevant to sex offenders with a learning disability? *Journal of Learning Disabilities and Offending Behaviour, 1*(3), 33–39. https://doi.org/10.5042/jldob.2010.0627

Barnao, M., Ward, T., & Casey, S. (2015). Looking beyond the illness: Forensic service users' perceptions of rehabilitation. *Journal of Interpersonal Violence, 30*, 1025–1045. https://doi.org/10.1177/0886260514539764

Barnao, M., Ward, T., & Casey, S. (2016). Taking the good life to the institution: Forensic service users' perceptions of the good lives model. *International Journal of Offender Therapy and Comparative Criminology, 60*, 766–786. https://doi.org/10.1177/0306624X15570027

Beech, A. R., & Ward, T. (2004). The integration of etiology and risk in sexual offenders: A theoretical framework. *Aggression and Violent Behavior, 10*(1), 31–63. https://doi.org/10.1016/j.avb.2003.08.002

Blair, R. J. J. (2013). The neurobiology of psychopathic traits in youths. *Nature Reviews Neuroscience, 14*, 786–799. https://doi.org/10.1038/nrn3577

Bonta, J., & Andrews, D. A. (2017). *The psychology of criminal conduct* (6th ed.). New York, NY: Routledge.

Chu, C. M., Koh, L. L., Zeng, G., & Teoh, J. (2015). Youth who sexual offended: Primary human goods and offense pathways. *Sexual Abuse: A Journal of Research and Treatment, 27*, 151–172. https://doi.org/10.1177/1079063213499188

Collaborative Outcome Data Committee. (2007). *Sex offender treatment outcome research: Guidelines for evaluation (CODC Guidelines), Part 1: Introduction and overview (corrections user report no 2007–002)*. Ottawa, ON, Canada: Public Safety Canada.

Cording, J. R., Beggs Christofferson, S. M., & Grace, R. C. (2016). Challenges for the theory and application of dynamic risk factors. *Psychology, Crime & Law, 22*(1–2), 84–103. https://doi.org/10.1080/1068316x.2015.1111367

Di Lorito, C., Völlm, B., & Dening, T. (2018). Psychiatric disorders among older prisoners: A systematic review and comparison study against older people in the community. *Aging & Mental Health, 22*(1), 1–10. https://doi.org/10.1080/13607863.2017.1286453

Dowden, C., & Andrews, D. A. (2000). Effective correctional treatment and violent reoffending: A meta-analysis. *Canadian Journal of Criminology, 42*, 449.

Duwe, G., & Rocque, M. (2016). A Jack of all trades but a master of none? Evaluating the performance of the level of service inventory–revised (LSI-R) in the assessment of risk and need. *Corrections, 1*(2), 81–106. https://doi.org/10.1080/23774657.2015.1111743

Farrall, S. (2005). On the existential aspects of desistance from crime. *Symbolic Interaction, 28*(3), 367–386. https://doi.org/10.1525/si.2005.28.issue-3
Fortune, C. A. (2017). The good lives model: A strength-based approach for youth offenders. *Aggression and Violent Behavior, 38*, 21–30. https://doi.org/10.1016/j.avb.2017.11.003
Fortune, C.-A., & Heffernan, R. (2019). The psychology of criminal conduct: criticisms and future directions. *Psychology, Crime & Law, 25*(6), 659–674. https://doi.org/10.1080/1068316X.2018.1560445
Gannon, T., King, T., Miles, H., Lockerbie, L., & Willis, G. M. (2011). Good lives sexual offender treatment for mentally disordered offenders. *British Journal of Forensic Practice, 13*(3), 153–168. https://doi.org/10.1108/14636641111157805
Gannon, T. A., Olver, M. E., Mallion, J. S., & James, M. (2019). Does specialized psychological treatment for offending reduce recidivism? A meta-analysis examining staff and program variables as predictors of treatment effectiveness. *Clinical Psychology Review, 73*, 101752. https://doi.org/10.1016/j.cpr.2019.101752
Grady, M. D., Edwards, D., Jr., & Pettus-Davis, C. (2017). A longitudinal outcome evaluation of a prison-based sex offender treatment program. *Sexual Abuse, 29*(3), 239–266. https://doi.org/10.1177/1079063215585731
Hannah-Moffat, K. (2016). A conceptual kaleidoscope: Contemplating 'dynamic structural risk' and an uncoupling of risk from need. *Psychology, Crime & Law, 22*(1–2), 33–46. https://doi.org/10.1080/1068316X.2015.1114115
Hanson, R. K., Bourgon, G., Helmus, L., & Hodgson, S. (2009). The principles of effective correctional treatment also apply to sexual offenders: A meta-analysis. *Criminal Justice and Behavior, 36*(9), 865–891. https://doi.org/10.1177/0093854809338545
Hart, S. D., & Logan, C. (2011). Formulation of violent risk using evidence-based assessments: The structured professional judgment approach. In P. Sturmey & M. McMurran (Eds.), *Forensic case formulation* (pp. 3–32). West Sussex, UK: Wiley.
Hart, S. D., Sturmey, P., Logan, C., & McMurran, M. (2011). Forensic case formulation. *International Journal of Forensic Mental Health, 10*, 118–126. https://doi.org/10.1080/14999013.2011.577137
Heffernan, R., Ward, T., Vandevelde, S., & Van Damme, L. (2019). Dynamic risk factors and constructing explanations of offending: The risk-causality method. *Aggression and Violent Behavior, 44*, 47–56. https://doi.org/10.1016/j.avb.2018.11.009
Heffernan, R., Wegerhoff, D., & Ward, T. (2019). Dynamic risk factors: Conceptualization, measurement, and evidence. *Aggression and Violent Behavior, 48*, 6–16. https://doi.org/10.1016/j.avb.2019.06.004
Hough, M. (2010). Gold standard or fool's gold? The pursuit of certainty in experimental criminology. *Criminology & Criminal Justice, 10*(1), 11–22. https://doi.org/10.1177/1748895809352597
Jung, S., & Gulayets, M. (2011). Using clinical variables to evaluate treatment effectiveness in programmes for sexual offenders. *Journal of Sexual Aggression, 17*(2), 166–180. https://doi.org/10.1080/13552601003802238
Kroner, D. G., Polaschek, D. L., Serin, R. C., & Skeem, J. L. (2017). An exploration of the symmetry between crime-causing and crime-reducing factors: Implications for delivery of offender services. *Psychological Services, 16*(2), 329–339. https://doi.org/10.1037/ser0000199
Langlands, R. L., Ward, T., & Gilchrist, E. (2009). Applying the good lives model to male perpetrators of domestic violence. *Behaviour Change, 26*(2), 113–129. https://doi.org/10.1375/bech.26.2.113
Laws, D. R., & Ward, T. (2011). *Desistance from sex offending: Alternatives to throwing away the keys*. New York, NY: Guilford.
Leaming, N., & Willis, G. M. (2016). The good lives model: New avenues for Māori rehabilitation? *Sexual Abuse in Australia and New Zealand, 7*, 59–69.
Mann, R. E., Hanson, R. K., & Thornton, D. (2010). Assessing risk for sexual recidivism: Some proposals on the nature of psychologically meaningful risk factors. *Sexual Abuse, 22*(2), 191–217. https://doi.org/10.1177/1079063210366039

Marsh, A. A., Finger, E. C., Fowler, K. A., Adalio, C. J., Jurkowitz, I. T., Schechter, J. C., … Blair, R. J. R. (2013). Empathic responsiveness in amygdala and anterior cingulate cortex in youths with psychopathic traits. *Journal of Child Psychology and Psychiatry, 54*(8), 900–910. https://doi.org/10.1111/jcpp.12063

Marshall, W. L., Marshall, L. E., Serran, G. A., & O'Brien, M. D. (2011). *Rehabilitating sexual offenders: A strength-based approach*. Washington, DC: American Psychological Association.

Newsome, J., & Cullen, F. T. (2017). The risk-need-responsivity model revisited: Using biosocial criminology to enhance offender rehabilitation. *Criminal Justice and Behavior, 44*(8), 1030–1049. https://doi.org/10.1177/0093854817715289

Polaschek, D. L. (2016). Desistance and dynamic risk factors belong together. *Psychology, Crime & Law, 22*(1–2), 171–189. https://doi.org/10.1080/1068316X.2015.1114114

Polaschek, D. L. L. (2012). An appraisal of the risk–need–responsivity (RNR) model of offender rehabilitation and its application in correctional treatment. *Legal and Criminological Psychology, 17*(1), 1–17. https://doi.org/10.1111/j.2044-8333.2011.02038.x

Purvis, M., & Ward, T. (2020). The good lives model of rehabilitation. In R. Salisbury (Ed.), *Free to be children: Preventing child sexual abuse in Aotearoa New Zealand*. Auckland, New Zealand: Massey University Press.

Purvis, M., Ward, T., & Willis, G. (2011). The good lives model in practice: Offence pathways and case management. *European Journal of Probation, 3*(2), 4–28. https://doi.org/10.1177/206622031100300202

Seligman, M. E., Railton, P., Baumeister, R. F., & Sripada, C. (2013). Navigating into the future or driven by the past. *Perspectives on Psychological Science, 8*(2), 119–141. https://doi.org/10.1177/1745691612474317

Seligman, M. E. P., Railton, P., Baumeister, R. R., & Sripada, C. (2016). *Homo prospectus*. New York, NY: Oxford University Press.

Serin, R. C., & Lloyd, C. D. (2009). Examining the process of offender change: The transition to crime desistance. *Psychology, Crime & Law, 15*(4), 347–364. https://doi.org/10.1080/10683160802261078

Serin, R. C., Lloyd, C. D., Helmus, L., Derkzen, D. M., & Luong, D. (2013). Does intra-individual change predict offender recidivism? Searching for the holy grail in assessing offender change. *Aggression and Violent Behavior, 18*(1), 32–53. https://doi.org/10.1016/j.avb.2012.09.002

Smallbone, S., & Cale, J. (2016). Situational theories. In A. R. Beech & T. Ward (Eds.), *The Wiley handbook on the theories, assessment, & treatment of sexual offending. Volume 1: Theories*. Hoboken, NJ: Wiley.

Sturmey, P., & McMurran, M. (Eds.). (2011). *Forensic case formulation*. Oxford, UK: Wiley-Blackwell.

Sullivan, J. A. (2019). Achieving cumulative progress in understanding crime: Some insights from the philosophy of science. *Psychology, Crime & Law, 25*(6), 561–576. https://doi.org/10.1080/1068316X.2019.1572755

Taylor, E. (2017). 'I should have been a security consultant': The good lives model and residential burglars. *European Journal of Criminology, 14*(4), 434–450. https://doi.org/10.1177/1477370816661743

Thakker, J., & Ward, T. (2010). The good lives model and the treatment of substance abusers. *Behaviour Change, 27*(3), 154–175. https://doi.org/10.1375/bech.27.3.154

Van Damme, L., Hoeve, M., Vermeiren, R., Vanderplasschen, W., & Colins, O. F. (2016). Quality of life in relation to future mental health problems and offending: Testing the good lives model among detained girls. *Law and Human Behavior, 40*, 285–294. https://doi.org/10.1037/lhb0000177

Wainwright, L., & Nee, C. (2014). The good lives model – New directions for preventative practice with children. *Psychology, Crime & Law, 20*(2), 166–182. https://doi.org/10.1080/1068316X.2013.770851

Ward, T. (2002a). Good lives and the rehabilitation of sexual offenders: Promises and problems. *Aggression and Violent Behavior, 7*, 513–528. https://doi.org/10.1016/S1359-1789(01)00076-3

Ward, T. (2002b). The management of risk and the design of good lives. *Australian Psychologist, 37*, 172–179. https://doi.org/10.1080/00050060210001706846
Ward, T. (2019). Why theory matters in correctional psychology. *Aggression and Violent Behavior, 48*, 36–45. https://doi.org/10.1016/j.avb.2019.08.015
Ward, T., & Beech, A. R. (2015). Dynamic risk factors: A theoretical dead-end? *Psychology. Crime & Law, 21*(2), 100–113. https://doi.org/10.1080/1068316x.2014.917854
Ward, T., & Fisher, D. D. (2005). New ideas in the treatment of sexual offenders. In W. L. Marshall, Y. Fernandez, L. Marshall, & G. A. Serran (Eds.), *Sexual offender treatment: Issues and controversies* (pp. 143–148). Hoboken, NJ: Wiley.
Ward, T., & Fortune, C.-A. (2016). The role of dynamic risk factors in the explanation of offending. *Aggression and Violent Behavior, 29*, 79–88. https://doi.org/10.1016/j.avb.2016.06.007
Ward, T., Mann, R. E., & Gannon, T. A. (2007). The good lives model of offender rehabilitation: Clinical implications. *Aggression and Violent Behavior, 12*(1), 87–107. https://doi.org/10.1016/j.avb.2006.03.004
Ward, T., & Maruna, S. (2007). *Rehabilitation: Beyond the risk paradigm*. London, UK: Routledge.
Ward, T., Melser, J., & Yates, P. M. (2007). Reconstructing the risk-need-responsivity model: A theoretical elaboration and evaluation. *Aggression and Violent Behavior, 12*(2), 208–228. https://doi.org/10.1016/j.avb.2006.07.001
Ward, T., Polaschek, D. L., & Beech, A. R. (2006). *Theories of sexual offending* (Vol. 21). Chichester, UK: Wiley.
Ward, T., & Stewart, C. A. (2003). The treatment of sex offenders: Risk management and good lives. *Professional Psychology: Research and Practice, 34*, 353–360. https://doi.org/10.1037/0735-7028.34.4.353
Ward, T., Wilshire, C., & Jackson, L. (2018). The contribution of neuroscience to forensic explanation. *Psychology, Crime & Law, 24*(3), 195–209. https://doi.org/10.1080/1068316X.2018.1427746
Weerasekera, P. (1996). *Multiperspective case formulation: A step towards treatment integration*. Malabar, FL: Krieger Publishing.
Whitehead, P. R., Ward, T., & Collie, R. M. (2007). Time for a change: Applying the good lives model of rehabilitation to a high-risk violent offender. *International Journal of Offender Therapy and Comparative Criminology, 51*, 578–598. https://doi.org/10.1177/0306624X06296236
Willis, G. M., & Ward, T. (2013). The good lives model: Does it work? Preliminary evidence. In *What works in offender rehabilitation: An evidence-based approach to assessment and treatment* (pp. 305–317). Chichester, UK: Wiley.
Willis, G. M., Ward, T., & Levenson, J. S. (2014). The good lives model (GLM): An evaluation of GLM operationalization in North American treatment programs. *Sexual Abuse: A Journal of Research & Treatment, 26*, 58–81. https://doi.org/10.1177/1079063213478202
Willis, G. M., Yates, P. M., Gannon, T. A., & Ward, T. (2013). How to integrate the good lives model into treatment programs for sexual offending: An introduction and overview. *Sexual Abuse, 25*(2), 123–142. https://doi.org/10.1177/1079063212452618
Wylie, L. A., & Griffin, H. L. (2013). G-map's application of the good lives model to adolescent males who sexually harm: A case study. *Journal of Sexual Aggression, 19*(3), 345–356. https://doi.org/10.1080/13552600.2011.650715
Yates, P. M., Prescott, D. S., & Ward, T. (2010). *Applying the good lives and self-regulation models to sex offender treatment: A practical guide for clinicians*. Brandon, VT: Safer Society Press.

Chapter 5
Conclusions and Future Directions

Abstract It has been suggested that a reformulation of dynamic risk factors (DRF) is a potential way forward to develop more comprehensive and mechanistic explanations of offending. The proposed benefits of this include more individualized and targeted treatment which is able to tap into the causal processes which influence behavior. In this chapter we summarize the contributions of each of the chapters in this book and then offer some concluding comments and suggestions to move the field towards a deeper and more comprehensive explanation of offending. Relying on DRF is not enough and is likely to result in research and practice dead ends.

Keywords Risk assessment · Dynamic risk factors · Boundary objects · Protective factors

Dynamic Risk Factors (DRF) are the most utilized concepts in the field of forensic and correctional practice. They provide the theoretical foundation of the RNR model and are the identified targets of correctional prevention programs, treatment programs, and probation services. Unfortunately, we know little about these important constructs and they have been largely ignored from a theoretical viewpoint by correctional researchers (for exceptions see Heffernan & Ward, 2017; Ward & Fortune, 2016a, 2016b). This book has built and expanded upon recent critical attention towards these constructs and questioned widespread assumptions concerning their relationship with risk and recidivism. We have provided a reformulation of DRF and offending as boundary objects and features of norm- and law-violating agency processes, and made some preliminary suggestions concerning what this means for practice moving forward. We will now summarize the contributions of each chapter and conclude with some suggestions for future research.

In Chap. 1 we provided an overview of the dominant conceptualization of DRF and their dual roles in practice, both as predictors of recidivism and targets for

R. Heffernan, T. Ward, *Dynamic Risk Factors for Sexual Offending: Causal Considerations*, SpringerBriefs in Psychology,
https://doi.org/10.1007/978-3-030-58275-3_5

treatment. We outlined a number of theories of offending, including those based on DRF and more recent theories based on the concept of agency (i.e., the predictive agency model). We argued that the transportation of DRF from the realm of prediction to treatment and explanation relies upon their status as causes of offending. In Chap. 2 we explored their causal nature through considering conceptual issues and the empirical evidence concerning DRF change. This chapter outlined numerous conceptual problems and mixed support for the relationship between treatment, DRF change, and recidivism. Unfortunately, any promising evidence is undermined by methodological weaknesses and the fact that in order "to test hypotheses about the causes of sexual offending, we must not only demonstrate a causal relation between variables but must also have a clear and concise conceptualization of the construct of interest and be able to accurately measure it" (Nunes et al., 2019, p. 231). We currently do not have clear and universal definitions of DRF due to their vague, normative, and composite nature.

In Chap. 3 we discussed the issues with classification in the forensic field, in particular the focus on offence types and DRF to classify individuals into different groups. We concluded that these classification systems were not adequate to guide explanations of behavior as they were unable to facilitate inductive inferences, they are not natural or scientific kinds. We then reiterated that in their current state DRF are unable to function as causes of offending and compared them against a list of causal criteria. We demonstrated that while DRF may predict and precede offending, they do not display the relationships with recidivism that you would expect from causal factors (i.e., following changes through treatment) and they lack coherence and specificity. This means that they are unable to pinpoint causal mechanisms as they are normatively defined composite categories. They contain a range of things (i.e., mental states, contexts, behaviors) and are only considered DRF due to their co-occurrence with crime (i.e., many of them are also present in non-offending populations). Due to these issues, we argued for an initial shift in focus from explaining DRF and crime, to explaining goal-directed behaviors (some of which are crimes). We outlined a number of suggestions for theory development, including the use of exemplars to sketch out the targets of explanation, a view of DRF as boundary objects which can be separated into different aspects (i.e., the agent-action-context schema) and the use of integrative pluralism to link local models.

In Chap. 4 we presented an approach to research building upon several recent suggestions for theory development. The risk-causality-method (RCM), suggests breaking DRF down, extracting their possible causal components, and then developing local models of these causal processes across multiple levels of analysis. The result is a set of local models which can be integrated within a model of agency. We then discussed some implications of the agency (i.e., the PAM) and RCM approaches for forensic practice. We proposed that by integrating the most promising aspects of the RNR, GLM, and future research building on the PAM and RCM, we can improve upon existing approaches to treatment and more readily meet the aims of the criminal justice system.

5.1 Future Directions

The main suggestion we will put forward for future research is that researchers utilize a methodological framework such as the RCM to guide the decomposition and exploration of crime-related problems (i.e., DRF). In addition, the use of agency theories within case formulation and treatment should eventually be expanded upon through the development of clear guidelines for practice. This will ensure that these concepts are used consistently and as intended. Relatedly, it is necessary to investigate the potential utility of future theories in informing correctional treatment and management of individuals within the community. This is a particularly important task because (once expanded upon) agency theories have the potential to improve practitioners' and participants' understanding of the causes of offending, enhance the therapeutic relationship, and ultimately to promote behavioral change in a more meaningful and enduring way. Our hope is that this approach will eventually offer a view of criminal behavior that capitalizes on decades of research into the nature of human functioning, rather than seeing those who engage in offending as fundamentally different to the rest of society. In our opinion, this shift is overdue, and is one way forward in response to the theoretical dead end the field has recently encountered.

The formulation of DRF from an agency perspective has a number of theoretical and practice advantages. First, viewing DRF as boundary objects means that researchers from different fields or working at varying levels of analysis accept that they are all investigating the same objects, and can coordinate their methods and models accordingly. Second, the stress on agency coheres with contemporary theoretical approaches in related scientific disciplines such as biology, criminology, and cognitive neuroscience: individuals are embodied, embedded, and enactive beings who construct and are shaped by their social and physical environments in ways that reflect their core interests and goals (Dent, Nielsen, & Ward, 2020). Third, this approach aligns well with current therapeutic innovations in the forensic psychology and criminal justice fields such as the emphasis on promoting strengths and a growing appreciation of the important role of cultural factors in creating "minds" (Heyes, 2018) and modulating risk (Schmidt, Heffernan, & Ward, 2020).

From a research viewpoint, examples of testable predictions derived from an agency persepctive (and future theories developed according to the RCM) include the following: (1) once broken down into *functional units,* DRF should shift in ways that reflect progress or no change across the offence and treatment process; (2) the manipulation of emotional states should result in shifts in cognitive factors and behaviors in the predicted directions; away or towards increased risky decisions (e.g., computer simulation studies); (3) the use of an agency formulation is expected to improve the quality of clinicians' case formulations compared to those relying on the standard characterizations of DRF; and (4) because individuals are hypothesized to use local (i.e., situation specific) models to predict outcomes and guide action it is expected that features of environments will strongly influence decision-making. It is also possible that measures of agency from other domains (e.g., poverty and empowerment, see Ibrahim & Alkire, 2007) can inform the investigation of predictive agency (e.g., control, efficacy, and autonomy) in relation to the experiences of forensic populations. Thus, future research requires a multi-disciplinary approach, and the integration of a range of explanations with various targets and levels of analysis.

As mentioned earlier, Sullivan (2019) suggests that inter-field cooperation is required in order to move towards a more comprehensive understanding of crime and related constructs. This involves researchers clearly defining and operationalizing constructs, and communicating across fields in order to add depth to our understanding. In order to integrate various levels of explanation, researchers must spell out the links between levels—for example, specifying the relationship between biological and psychological mechanisms and how they might give rise to behaviors. This is no easy task; researchers have long struggled to elucidate the relationship between these levels of analysis, and as Thomas and Sharp (2019) state:

> … this lack of understanding regarding how to relate psychology to biology is a major reason for the dearth of causal explanations of psychopathology. Although this issue remains unresolved, field-wide attention has been primarily focused on whether findings are reproducible. Demonstrating reproducibility, however, does not suffice for building strong causal theories. A highly stable correlation between an intervention and an outcome may do little in explaining why the treatment works, which is necessary to further advance for whom and under what conditions it works best. In general, causal theories are vital to improving predictions regarding how psychological processes unfold under various conditions and creating more precise interventions on psychological functions that go awry across various forms of psychopathology. (p. 2)

These issues highlighted in the field of psychopathology are analogous to the lack of causal explanations in forensic psychology. This further necessitates inter-field co-ordination to provide depth to explanations of offending, as proposed by Sullivan (2019), and highlights the complexity of this research.

Relatedly, recent attempts have been made to elaborate upon the theoretical basis of the RNR. For example, enhancing the model through integrating biological and social explanations (Carter & Mann, 2016; Newsome & Cullen, 2017). We suggest that this research is a step in the right direction when it comes to developing multilevel explanations of crime, and that it may offer additional areas for inquiry in research frameworks such as the RCM. In addition, it has been suggested that of the core RNR principles, responsivity is "the least developed of the three. It is theoretically unsophisticated: a catch-all category" (Polaschek, 2012, p. 8). Thus, we believe it is crucial that future research prioritise the elaboration of this principle, as it encompasses important issues such as motivation and cultural needs. A more comprehensive understanding of the perspectives and priorities (i.e., core goals, interests) of potential participants can help practitioners overcome problems such as high rates of drop-out and poor engagement. In addition, while criminogenic targets *can be* framed positively (Polaschek, 2012), they are still an externally imposed list of treatment goals that are not routinely linked with personally meaningful outcomes other than the potential consequences of reoffending (i.e., future prison sentences). It would be useful to look at the impact of language and orientation of treatment goals on participants' expectations of treatment, subsequent engagement, and other meaningful outcomes (i.e., PHG attainment). Questions which would enhance our understanding of what works include: why do people change? Which aspects of treatment are most useful to individuals who want to change? What sorts of changes are most important in reducing risk? And which internal and external resources best support the process of desistance from offending? The answers to these questions can help us to develop more balanced approaches to treatment, where the process of change is considered as important as the focus on past behavior and likelihood of future harms.

In addition, we suggest that desistance research may be able to provide answers to some of these questions. Briefly, desistance may be defined as the on-going process of shifting from active offending to reductions in and eventually the cessation of offending altogether. Features which have been observed to precede or facilitate this process include marriage, employment, and the development of a new prosocial identity (McAlinden, Farmer, & Maruna, 2017). The desistance research also suggests that the development of a coherent narrative explaining why the offence occurred and why it will not happen again can help an individual to make sense of their past and take control of their future (Maruna, 2011). Agency and autonomy are necessary for individuals to take control of their future and develop the internal and external resources necessary to make shifts in identity and attain needs in prosocial ways. The resources associated with desistance (e.g., relationships, employment, self-control, good problem-solving skills) are often referred to as protective factors (PF), and we currently lack an adequate understanding of how they function to reduce risk (Ward, 2017).

We suggest that the future development of agency theories and local models of capacities can help us understand the relationship between risk and PF. The concepts of PHG and agency capacities can enhance our understanding of how PF or desistance events such as employment and relationships can reduce risk, and why their influence may vary across individuals and situations. For example, employment could be thought of as a secondary good which meets a range of needs, including (but not limited to) excellence in work and a sense of achievement, agency, life (i.e., financial resources), and inner peace (i.e., freedom from stress). Employment may also be a result of the development or strengthening of agency capacities such as conscientiousness, self-control, communication skills, and so on. Employment which does not reflect these strengths or meet these PHG is less likely to support desistance and may lead to the use of other secondary goods (e.g., substance abuse, theft, dishonesty). The use of a GLP in treatment can be linked with possible futures within the desistance literature. For example, individuals must be able to conceive of a personally meaningful and attainable future and construct a new identity—"the self is continually being projected into the future" (Farrall, 2005, p. 369). This is a key commitment of the predictive agency perspective (i.e., the mind as a predictive engine), and in this sense models such as the PAM can be used equally to explain offending and desistance. It can help us understand the reasons for change and how this process might occur, for example, what needs are motivating change and what resources does a person require.

We suggest that when it comes to informing interventions and explaining prosocial change, neither DRF nor PF on their own can provide the full picture—both offer one source of information concerning an individual's ability to meet their needs in prosocial ways. What is needed is a model that can account for why we observe DRF and PF alongside various behavioral patterns or trajectories of crime and desistance. We suggest that agentic perspectives can do this through their focus on goal-directed behavior generally, rather than value-laden outcomes. Thus, research into the desistance process can provide useful targets for explanation and intervention and it may also provide useful starting points for research into the mechanisms underpinning desistance and thus should eventually be included alongside DRF as instigators of inquiry in the RCM.

Finally we propose that future research should aim to elaborate upon why some individuals choose offending as a means to meet their needs, while others do not. This may be done by elaborating upon the development and maintenance of an individual's general and specific models and their role in action selection. For example, how are these formed and how can they change? Do they represent enduring models (i.e., sexual offending is always an option) or temporary impairments? It is a general weakness of previous theories that they fail to specify why some people use sexual offending to meet needs (i.e., for intimacy, pleasure, control), while others choose other more or less adaptive behaviors. It is likely that this is due to past experiences and expectations available to draw from during planning for action, and that these differ across individuals. These processes can be investigated via in-depth interviews with individuals who have committed sexual offences (or other behaviors) which may help researchers to understand the development and revision of these models over time. For example, by asking questions about early sexual experiences and the frequency of thoughts about sexual offending (i.e., the availability of general models supporting sexual offending). In addition, researchers could look at the differences between the planning abilities (i.e., generation and selection of options) for individuals who have sexually offended and individuals who are motivated for sexual offending against children but refrain from acting on these preferences (e.g., non-offending individuals with pedophilic interests). This would help researchers to better understand the relationship between sexual preferences, motivation, and planning.

5.2 Final Conclusions

To conclude this book, we return to the two questions set out in the preface. What role, if any, should DRF play in the development of explanations of crime (and reoffending)? And how can they assist practitioners in treatment? Hopefully the reader is left with a sense that while DRF are useful for prediction, they are themselves not explanations for crime. However, due to their frequent (but varied) co-existence with the behaviors we wish to prevent, they can play an important methodological function within research frameworks such as the RCM. When deconstructed, DRF provide clues which can lead us to a range of potential causal mechanisms which can interact to explain any occurrence of behavior, including norm-violations such as crime. These causal mechanisms can then be investigated and fleshed out across multiple levels of explanation, and then integrated with other mechanisms within a model of human behavior (i.e., the PAM). The end point being a comprehensive multi-level model which can be applied to any number of problems (i.e., exemplars in research, individuals in treatment).

We believe that the reconceptualization of DRF developed throughout this book has the potential to take the field of forensic psychology in a new direction and prevent us from encountering an otherwise likely theoretical dead end. We have argued that the standard focus on DRF as explanations for offending falls short of causal explanation and that these constructs suffer from a number of conceptual problems. By shifting the focus from lists of correlates to the mechanisms underpinning goal-directed behavior, researchers can develop explanations which include normative aspects of human functioning, such as values, motivation, and reflection. They may then pinpoint the source of any impairments in functioning, but also view behavior in light of norms as well as contextual opportunities and constraints. As well as a promising way forward for theory development, this offers up exciting new opportunities for treatment. We have suggested that agency theories may do this through adding depth to rehabilitation models such as the GLM. Then local models may be developed which add further depth through specifying the internal and external resources which are required for both the attainment of needs and reduction of risk, and thus which should be included as treatment goals. The recent introduction of the concept of boundary objects will hopefully anchor this work on crime while also extending the horizon of forensic researchers and practitioners to the full range of human needs and goals.

It is hoped that these innovations will eventually filter through to the design and delivery of treatment programs which are more individualized and capable of motivating prosocial change. After all, what good is a theory of offending if it does not have a positive impact on the lives of those who engage in and are affected by crime? We must not forget that, like us, persons who have committed crimes are motivated towards valued outcomes and experiences. Only when we understand individuals within the criminal justice system as people like us can we work alongside them to develop the resources they require to live more fulfilling and less harmful lives.

References

Carter, A. J., & Mann, R. E. (2016). Organizing principles for an integrated model of change for the treatment of sexual offending. In A. R. Beech & T. Ward (Eds.), *The Wiley handbook on the theories, assessment and treatment of sexual offending* (Vol. Vol. 1, pp. 359–381). Chichester, UK: Wiley. https://doi.org/10.1002/9781118574003.wattso017

Dent, H., Nielsen, K., & Ward, T. (2020). Correctional rehabilitation and human functioning: An embodied, embedded, and enactive approach. *Aggression and Violent Behavior, 51*. https://doi.org/10.1016/j.avb.2020.101383

Farrall, S. (2005). On the existential aspects of desistance from crime. *Symbolic Interaction, 28*(3), 367–386. https://doi.org/10.1525/si.2005.28.issue-3
Heffernan, R., & Ward, T. (2017). A comprehensive theory of dynamic risk and protective factors. *Aggression and Violent Behavior, 37*, 129–141. https://doi.org/10.1016/j.avb.2017.10.003
Heyes, C. (2018). *Cognitive gadgets: The cultural evolution of thinking*. Cambridge, MA: Harvard University Press.
Ibrahim, S., & Alkire, S. (2007). Agency and empowerment: A proposal for internationally comparable indicators. *Oxford Development Studies, 35*(4), 379–403. https://doi.org/10.1080/13600810701701897
Maruna, S. (2011). Reentry as a rite of passage. *Punishment & Society, 13*(1), 3–28. https://doi.org/10.1177/1462474510385641
McAlinden, A. M., Farmer, M., & Maruna, S. (2017). Desistance from sexual offending: Do the mainstream theories apply? *Criminology & Criminal Justice, 17*(3), 266–283. https://doi.org/10.1177/1748895816670201
Newsome, J., & Cullen, F. T. (2017). The risk-need-responsivity model revisited: Using biosocial criminology to enhance offender rehabilitation. *Criminal Justice and Behavior, 44*(8), 1030–1049. https://doi.org/10.1177/0093854817715289
Nunes, K. L., Pedneault, C. I., Filleter, W. E., Maimone, S., Blank, C., & Atlas, M. (2019). "I know correlation doesn't prove causation, but…": Are we jumping to unfounded conclusions about the causes of sexual offending? *Sexual Abuse, 31*(2), 220–236. https://doi.org/10.1177/1079063217729156
Polaschek, D. L. L. (2012). An appraisal of the risk–need–responsivity (RNR) model of offender rehabilitation and its application in correctional treatment. *Legal and Criminological Psychology, 17*(1), 1–17. https://doi.org/10.1111/j.2044-8333.2011.02038.x
Schmidt, S., Heffernan, R., & Ward, T. (2020). Why we cannot explain cross-cultural differences in risk assessment. *Aggression and Violent Behavior, 50*, 1–12. https://doi.org/10.1016/j.avb.2019.101346
Sullivan, J. A. (2019). Achieving cumulative progress in understanding crime: Some insights from the philosophy of science. *Psychology, Crime & Law, 25*(6), 561–576. https://doi.org/10.1080/1068316X.2019.1572755
Thomas, J. G., & Sharp, P. B. (2019). Mechanistic science: A new approach to comprehensive psychopathology research that relates psychological and biological phenomena. *Clinical Psychological Science, 7*(2), 196–215. https://doi.org/10.1177/2167702618810223
Ward, T. (2017). Prediction and agency: The role of protective factors in correctional rehabilitation and desistance. *Aggression and Violent Behavior, 32*, 19–28. https://doi.org/10.1016/j.avb.2016.11.012
Ward, T., & Fortune, C.-A. (2016a). The role of dynamic risk factors in the explanation of offending. *Aggression and Violent Behavior, 29*, 79–88. https://doi.org/10.1016/j.avb.2016.06.007
Ward, T., & Fortune, C.-A. (2016b). From dynamic risk factors to causal processes: A methodological framework. *Psychology, Crime & Law, 22*(1–2), 190–202. https://doi.org/10.1080/1068316x.2015.1117080

MIX
Papier aus verantwortungsvollen Quellen
Paper from responsible sources
FSC® C105338

If you have any concerns about our products,
you can contact us on
ProductSafety@springernature.com

In case Publisher is established outside the EU,
the EU authorized representative is:
Springer Nature Customer Service Center GmbH
Europaplatz 3, 69115 Heidelberg, Germany

Printed by Libri Plureos GmbH
in Hamburg, Germany